The Book of Dragons

E. Nesbit

A WATERMILL CLASSIC

10 9 8 7 6 5 4 3 2 1

Contents

Chapter 1

The Book of Beasts

He happened to be building a palace when the news came, and he left all the bricks kicking about the floor for Nurse to clear up—but then the news was rather remarkable news. You see, there was a knock at the front door and voices talking downstairs, and Lionel thought it was the man come to see about the gas which had not been allowed to be lighted since the day when Lionel made a swing by tying his skipping rope to the gas bracket.

And then, quite suddenly, Nurse came in and said, "Master Lionel, dear, they've come to fetch you to go and be king."

Then she made haste to change his smock and to wash his face and hands and brush his hair, and all the time she was doing it Lionel kept wriggling and fidgeting and saying "Oh, don't, Nurse" and "I'm sure my ears are quite clean" or "Never mind my hair, it's all right" and "That'll do."

"You're going on as if you was going to be an eel instead of a king," said Nurse.

The moment Nurse let go for a moment Lionel bolted off without waiting for his clean handkerchief, and in the drawing room there were two very grave-looking gentlemen in red robes with fur, and gold coronets with velvet sticking up out of the middle like the cream in the very expensive jam tarts.

They bowed low to Lionel, and the gravest one said, "Sire, your great-great-great-great-great-grandfather, the king of this country, is dead, and now you have got to come and be king."

"Yes, please, sir," said Lionel. "When does it begin?"

"You will be crowned this afternoon," said the grave gentleman who was not quite so grave-looking as the other.

"Would you like me to bring Nurse, or what time would you like me to be fetched, and hadn't I better put on my velvet suit with the lace collar?" said Lionel, who had often been out to tea.

"Your nurse will be removed to the palace later. No, never mind about changing your suit—the royal robes will cover all that up."

The grave gentlemen led the way to a coach with eight white horses, which was drawn up in front of the house where Lionel lived. It was No. 7, on the left-hand side of the street as you go up.

Lionel ran upstairs at the last minute, and he kissed Nurse and said, "Thank you for washing me. I wish I'd let you do the other ear. No—there's no time now. Give me the hanky. Good-bye, Nurse."

2

"Good-bye, ducky," said Nurse. "Be a good little king, now, and say 'please' and 'thank you,' and remember to pass the cake to the little girls, and don't have more than two helps of anything."

So off went Lionel to be made a king. He had never expected to be a king any more than you have, so it was all quite new to him—so new that he had never even thought of it. And as the coach went through the town he had to bite his tongue to be quite sure it was real, because if his tongue was real it showed he wasn't dreaming. Half an hour before he had been building with bricks in the nursery, and now—the streets were all fluttering with flags, every window was crowded with people waving handkerchiefs and scattering flowers, there were scarlet soldiers everywhere along the pavements, and all the bells of all the churches were ringing like mad, and like a great song to the music of their ringing he heard thousands of people shouting "Long live Lionel! Long live our little king!"

He was a little sorry at first that he had not put on his best clothes, but he soon forgot to think about that. If he had been a girl he would very likely have bothered about it the whole time.

As they went along, the grave gentlemen, who were the chancellor and the prime minister, explained the things which Lionel did not understand.

"I thought we were a republic," said Lionel. "I'm sure there hasn't been a king for some time."

"Sire, your great-great-great-great-great-grandfather's death happened when my grandfather was a little boy," said the prime minister, "and since then your loyal people have been saving up to buy you a crown—so much a week, you know, according to people's means—sixpence a week from those who have first-rate pocket money, down to a halfpenny a week from those who haven't so much. You know it's the rule that the crown must be paid for by the people."

"But hadn't my great-great-however-much-it-is-grandfather a crown?"

"Yes, but he sent it to be tinned over, for fear of vanity, and he had had all the jewels taken out, and sold them to buy books. He was a strange man. A very good king he was, but he had his faults—he was fond of books. Almost with his latest breath he sent the crown to be tinned—and he never lived to pay the tinsmith's bill."

Here the prime minister wiped away a tear, and just then the carriage stopped and Lionel was taken out of the carriage to be crowned. Being crowned is much more tiring work than you would suppose, and by the time it was over, and Lionel had worn the royal robes for an hour or two and had had his hand kissed by everybody whose business it was to do it, he was quite worn out, and was very glad to get into the palace nursery.

Nurse was there, and tea was ready: seedy cake and plummy cake, and jam and hot buttered toast, and the prettiest china with red and gold and blue flowers on it, and real tea, and as many cups of it as you liked.

After tea Lionel said, "I think I should like a book. Will you get me one, Nurse?"

"Bless the child," said Nurse. "You don't suppose you've lost the use of your legs with just being a king? Run along, do, and get your books yourself."

So Lionel went down into the library. The prime minister and the chancellor were there, and when Lionel came in they bowed very low, and were beginning to ask Lionel most politely what on earth he was coming bothering for now —when Lionel cried out, "Oh, what a worldful of books! Are they yours?"

"They are yours, Your Majesty," answered the chancellor. "They were the property of the late king, your great-great—"

"Yes, I know," Lionel interrupted. "Well, I shall read them all. I love to read. I am so glad I learned to read."

"If I might venture to advise Your Majesty," said the prime minister, "I should *not* read these books. Your great—"

"Yes?" said Lionel quickly.

"He was a very good king—oh, yes, really a very superior king in his way, but he was a little —well, strange."

"Mad?" asked Lionel cheerfully.

"No, no"—both the gentlemen were sincerely shocked. "Not mad, but if I may express it so, he was—er—too clever by half. And I should not like a little king of mine to have anything to do with his books."

Lionel looked puzzled.

"The fact is," the chancellor went on, twisting his red beard in an agitated way, "your great—"

"Go on," said Lionel.

"Was *called* a wizard."

"But he wasn't?"

"Of course not—a most worthy king was your great—"

"I see."

"But I wouldn't touch his books."

"Just this one," cried Lionel, laying his hands on the cover of a great brown book that lay on the study table. It had gold patterns on the brown leather, and gold clasps with turquoises and rubies in the twists of them, and gold corners, so that the leather should not wear out too quickly.

"I *must* look at this one," Lionel said, for on the back in big letters he read, "*The Book of Beasts*."

The Chancellor said, "Don't be a silly little king."

But Lionel had got the gold clasps undone, and he opened the first page, and there was a beautiful butterfly all red and brown and yellow and blue, so beautifully painted that it looked as if it were alive.

"There," said Lionel, "isn't that lovely? Why—"

But as he spoke the beautiful butterfly fluttered its many-colored wings on the yellow old page of the book, and flew up and out of the window.

"Well!" said the prime minister, as soon as he could speak for the lump of wonder that had got into his throat and tried to choke him. "That's magic, that is."

But before he had spoken, the king had turned the next page, and there was a shining bird complete and beautiful in every blue feather of him. Under him was written "Blue Bird of Paradise," and while the king gazed enchanted at the charming picture the blue bird fluttered his wings on the yellow page and spread them and flew out of the book.

Then the prime minister snatched the book away from the king and shut it up on the blank page where the bird had been, and put it on a very high shelf.

And the chancellor gave the king a good shaking and said, "You're a naughty, disobedient little king," and was very angry indeed.

"I don't see that I've done any harm," said Lionel. He hated being shaken, as all the boys do. He would much rather have been slapped.

"No harm?" said the chancellor. "Ah—but what do you know about it? That's the question. How do you know what might have been on the next page—a snake or a worm, or a centipede or a revolutionist, or something like that."

"Well, I'm sorry if I've vexed you," said Lionel. "Come let's kiss and be friends." So he kissed the prime minister, and they settled down for a nice quiet game of noughts and crosses while the chancellor went to add up his accounts.

But when Lionel was in bed he could not sleep for thinking of the book, and when the full moon was shining with all her might and light he got up and crept down to the library and climbed up and got *The Book of Beasts*.

He took it outside onto the terrace, where the moonlight was as bright as day, and he opened the book, and saw the empty pages with "Butterfly" and "Blue Bird of Paradise"

7

underneath, and then he turned the next page. There was some sort of red thing sitting under a palm tree, and under it was written "Dragon." The dragon did not move, and the king shut up the book rather quickly and went back to bed.

But the next day he wanted another look, so he got the book out into the garden, and when he undid the clasps with the rubies and turquoises, the book opened all by itself at the picture with "Dragon" underneath, and the sun shone full on the page. And then, quite suddenly, a great red dragon came out of the book, and spread vast scarlet wings and flew away across the garden to the far hills, and Lionel was left with the empty page before him, for the page was quite empty except for the green palm tree and the yellow desert and the little streaks of red where the paint brush had gone outside the pencil outline of the red dragon.

And then Lionel felt that he had indeed done it. He had not been king twenty-four hours, and already he had let loose a red dragon to worry his faithful subjects' lives out. And they had been saving up so long to buy him a crown and everything!

Lionel began to cry.

Then the chancellor and the prime minister and the nurse all came running to see what was the matter. And when they saw the book they understood, and the chancellor said, "You naughty little king! Put him to bed, Nurse, and let him think over what he's done."

"Perhaps, My Lord," said the prime minister, "we'd better first find out just exactly what he has done."

Then Lionel, in floods of tears, said, "It's a red dragon, and it's gone flying away to the hills, and I am so sorry, and, oh, do forgive me!"

But the prime minister and the chancellor had other things to think of than forgiving Lionel. They hurried off to consult the police and see what could be done. Everyone did what they could. They sat on committees and stood on guard, and lay in wait for the dragon, but he stayed up in the hills, and there was nothing more to be done. The faithful nurse, meanwhile, did not neglect her duty. Perhaps she did more than anyone else, for she slapped the king and put him to bed without his tea, and when it got dark she would not give him a candle to read by.

"You are a naughty king," she said, "and nobody will love you."

Next day the dragon was still quiet, though the more poetic of Lionel's subjects could see the redness of the dragon shining through the green trees quite plainly. So Lionel put on his crown and sat on his throne and said he wanted to make some laws.

And I need hardly say that though the prime minister and the chancellor and the nurse might have the very poorest opinion of Lionel's private judgment, and might even slap him and send him to bed, the minute he got on his throne and set his crown on his head, he became infallible— which means that everything he said was right, and that he couldn't possibly make a mistake.

So when he said "There is to be a law forbidding people to open books in schools or elsewhere," he had the support of at least half of his subjects, and the other half—the grown-up half —pretended to think he was quite right.

Then he made a law that everyone should always have enough to eat. And this pleased everyone except the ones who had always had too much.

And when several other nice new laws were made and written down he went home and made mudhouses and was very happy. And he said to his nurse, "People will love me now I've made such a lot of pretty new laws for them."

But Nurse said, "Don't count your chickens, my dear. You haven't seen the last of that dragon yet."

Now, the next day was Saturday. And in the afternoon the dragon suddenly swooped down upon the common in all his hideous redness and carried off the football players, umpires, goalposts, football, and all.

Then the people were very angry indeed, and they said, "We might as well be a republic. After saving up all these years to get his crown and everything!"

And wise people shook their heads and foretold a decline in the National Love of Sport. And, indeed, football was not at all popular for some time afterwards.

Lionel did his best to be a good king during the week, and the people were beginning to forgive him for letting the dragon out of the book. "After all," they said, "football is a dangerous game, and perhaps it is wise to discourage it."

Popular opinion held that the football players, being tough and hard, had disagreed with the dragon so much that he had gone away to some place where they only play cat's cradle and games that do not make you hard and tough.

All the same, Parliament met on the Saturday afternoon, a convenient time, when most of the members would be free to attend, to consider the dragon. But unfortunately the dragon, who had only been asleep, woke up because it was Saturday, and he considered the Parliament, and afterwards there were not any members left, so they tried to make a new Parliament, but being an M.P. had somehow grown as unpopular as football playing, and no one would consent to be elected, so they had to do without a Parliament. When the next Saturday came round everyone was a little nervous, but the red dragon was pretty quiet that day and only ate an orphanage.

Lionel was very, very unhappy. He felt that it was his disobedience that had brought this trouble on the Parliament and the orphanage and the football players, and he felt that it was his duty to try and do something. The question was, what?

The blue bird that had come out of the book used to sing very nicely in the palace rose garden, and the butterfly was very tame and would perch on his shoulder when he walked among the tall lilies, so Lionel saw that all the creatures in *The Book of Beasts* could not be wicked, like the dragon, and he thought, "Suppose I could get another beast out who would fight the dragon?"

So he took *The Book of Beasts* out into the rose garden and opened the page next to the one where the dragon had been just a tiny bit to see what the name was. He could only see "cora," but he felt the middle of the page swelling up thick with the creature that was trying to come out, and it was only by putting the book down and sitting on it suddenly, very hard, that he managed to get it shut.

Then he fastened the clasps with the rubies and turquoises in them and sent for the chancellor, who had been ill on Saturday week, and so had not been eaten with the rest of the Parliament, and he said, "What animal ends in 'cora'?"

The chancellor answered, "The manticora, of course."

"What is he like?" asked the king.

"He is the sworn foe of dragons," said the chancellor. "He drinks their blood. He is yellow, with the body of a lion and the face of a man. I wish we had a few manticoras here now. But the last died hundreds of years ago—worse luck!"

Then the king ran and opened the book at the page that had "cora" on it, and there was the picture Manticora, all yellow, with a lion's body and a man's face, just as the chancellor had said. And under the picture was written, "Manticora."

And in a few minutes the manticora came sleepily out of the book, rubbing its eyes with its hands and mewing piteously. It seemed very stupid, and when Lionel gave it a push and said, "Go along and fight the dragon, do," it put its tail between its legs and fairly ran away. It went and hid behind the town hall, and at night when the people were asleep it went round and ate all the pussy cats in the town. And then it mewed more than ever. And on the Saturday morning, when people were a little timid about going out, because the dragon had no regular hour for calling, the manticora went up and down the streets and drank all the milk that was left in the cans at the doors for people's teas, and it ate the cans as well.

And just when it had finished the very last little ha'porth, which was short measure, because the milkman's nerves were quite upset, the red dragon came down the street looking for the manticora. It edged off when it saw him coming, for it was not at all the dragon-fighting kind, and seeing no other door open, the poor, hunted creature took refuge in the General Post Office, and there the dragon found it, trying to conceal itself among the ten o'clock mail. The dragon fell on the manticora at once, and the mail was no defense. The mewings were heard all over the town. All the pussies and the milk the manticora had had seemed to have strengthened its mew wonderfully. Then there was a sad silence, and presently the people whose windows looked that way saw the dragon come walking down the steps of the General Post Office spitting fire and smoke, together with tufts of manticora fur and the fragments of the registered letters. Things were growing very serious. However popular the king might become during the week, the dragon was sure to do something on Saturday to upset the people's loyalty.

The dragon was a perfect nuisance for the whole of Saturday, except during the hour of noon, and then he had to rest under a tree or he would have caught fire from the heat of the sun. You see, he was very hot to begin with.

At last came a Saturday when the dragon actually walked into the royal nursery and carried off the king's own pet rocking horse. Then the king cried for six days, and on the seventh he was so tired that he had to stop. Then

13

he heard the blue bird singing among the roses and saw the butterfly fluttering among the lilies, and he said, "Nurse, wipe my face, please. I am not going to cry anymore."

Nurse washed his face and told him not to be a silly little king. "Crying," said she, "never did anyone any good yet."

"I don't know," said the little king. "I seem to see better and to hear better now that I've cried for a week. Now, Nurse, dear, I know I'm right, so kiss me in case I never come back. I *must* try if I can't save the people."

"Well, if you must, you must," said Nurse, "but don't tear your clothes or get your feet wet."

So off he went.

The blue bird sang more sweetly than ever, and the butterfly shone more brightly, as Lionel once more carried *The Book of Beasts* out into the rose garden and opened it—very quickly, so that he might not be afraid and change his mind. The book fell open wide, almost in the middle, and there was written at the bottom of the page, "The Hippogriff." And before Lionel had time to see what the picture was, there was a fluttering of great wings and a stamping of hoofs, and a sweet, soft, friendly neighing, and there came out of the book a beautiful white horse with a long, long, white mane and a long, long, white tail, and he had great wings like swan's wings, and the softest, kindest eyes in the world, and he stood there among the roses.

The hippogriff rubbed its silky-soft, milky-white nose against the little king's shoulder, and the little king thought, "But for the wings you

are very like my poor, dear, lost rocking horse.''
And the blue bird's song was very loud and
sweet.

Then suddenly the king saw coming through
the sky the great straggling, sprawling, wicked
shape of the red dragon. And he knew at once
what he must do. He caught up *The Book of Beasts*
and jumped on the back of the gentle, beautiful
hippogriff, and leaning down he whispered in
the sharp white ear: ''Fly, dear hippogriff, fly
your very fastest to the Pebbly Waste.''

And when the dragon saw them start, he
turned and flew after them, with his great wings
flapping like clouds at sunset, and the
hippogriff's wide wings were snowy as clouds at
the moon-rising.

When the people in the town saw the dragon
fly off after the hippogriff and the king, they all
came out of their houses to look, and when they
saw the two disappear they made up their minds
to the worst, and began to think what would be
worn for court mourning.

But the dragon could not catch the hippogriff.
The red wings were bigger than the white ones,
but they were not so strong, and so the white-
winged horse flew away and away and away,
with the dragon pursuing, till he reached the
very middle of the Pebbly Waste.

Now, the Pebbly Waste is just like the parts of
the seaside where there is no sand—all round,
loose, shifting stones, and there is no grass there
and no tree within a hundred miles of it.

Lionel jumped off the white horse's back in
the very middle of the Pebbly Waste, and he
hurriedly unclasped *The Book of Beasts* and laid it

open on the pebbles. Then he clattered among the pebbles in his haste to get back onto his white horse, and had just jumped on when up came the dragon. He was flying very feebly and looking round everywhere for a tree, for it was just on the stroke of twelve, the sun was shining like a gold guinea[1] in the blue sky, and there was not a tree for a hundred miles.

The white-winged horse flew round and round the dragon as he writhed on the dry pebbles. He was getting very hot: indeed, parts of him even had begun to smoke. He knew that he must certainly catch fire in another minute unless he could get under a tree. He made a snatch with his red claws at the king and hippo-griff, but he was too feeble to reach them, and besides, he did not dare to overexert himself for fear he should get any hotter.

It was then that he saw *The Book of Beasts* lying on the pebbles, open at the page with "Dragon" written at the bottom. He looked and he hesitated, and he looked again, and then, with one last squirm of rage, the dragon wriggled himself back into the picture, and sat down under the palm tree, and the page was a little singed as he went in.

As soon as Lionel saw that the dragon had really been obliged to go and sit under his own palm tree because it was the only tree there, he jumped off his horse and shut the book with a bang.

"Oh, hurrah!" he cried. "Now we really *have* done it."

[1]*An English gold coin issued from 1663 to 1803 and fixed in 1717 at 21 shillings.*

And he clasped the book very tight with the turquoise and ruby clasps.

"Oh, my precious hippogriff," he cried, "you are the bravest, dearest, most beautiful—"

"Hush," whispered the hippogriff modestly. "Don't you see that we are not alone?"

And indeed there was quite a crowd round them on the Pebbly Waste: the prime minister and the Parliament and the football players and the orphanage and the manticora and the rocking horse, and indeed everyone who had been eaten by the dragon. You see, it was impossible for the dragon to take them into the book with him—it was a tight fit even for one dragon—so, of course, he had to leave them outside.

They all got home somehow, and all lived happily ever after.

When the king asked the manticora where he would like to live he begged to be allowed to go back into the book. "I do not care for public life," he said.

Of course he knew his way onto his own page, so there was no danger of his opening the book at the wrong page and letting out a dragon or anything. So he got back into his picture, and has never come out since. That is why you will never see a manticora as long as you live, except in a picture book. And of course he left the pussies outside, because there was no room for them in the book—and the milk cans too.

Then the rocking horse begged to be allowed to go and live on the hippogriff's page of the book. "I should like," he said, "to live somewhere where dragons can't get at me."

So the beautiful, white-winged hippogriff showed him the way in, and there he stayed till the king had him taken out for his great-great-great-great-grandchildren to play with.

As for the hippogriff, he accepted the position of the king's own rocking horse—a situation left vacant by the retirement of the wooden one. And the blue bird and the butterfly sing and flutter among the lilies and roses of the palace garden to this very day.

Chapter 2

Uncle James,
or the Purple Stranger

The princess and the gardener's boy were playing in the back yard.

"What will you do when you grow up, Princess?" asked the gardener's boy.

"I should like to marry you, Tom," said the princess. "Would you mind?"

"No," said the gardener's boy. "I shouldn't mind much. I'll marry you if you like—if I have time."

For the gardener's boy meant, as soon as he was grown-up, to be a general and a poet and a prime minister and an admiral and a civil engineer. Meanwhile, he was top of all his classes at school, and tiptop of the geography class.

As for the princess Mary Ann, she was a very good little girl, and everyone loved her. She was always kind and polite, even to her uncle James and to other people whom she did not like very much, and though she was not very clever, for a princess, she always tried to do her lessons. Even if you know perfectly well that you can't do your lessons, you may as well try, and sometimes you find that by some fortunate accident they really *are* done. Then the princess had a truly good heart: she was always kind to her pets. She never slapped her hippopotamus when it broke her dolls in its playful gambols, and she never forgot to feed her rhinoceroses in their little hutch in the back yard. Her elephant was devoted to her, and sometimes Mary Ann made her nurse quite cross by smuggling the dear little thing up to bed with her and letting it go to sleep with its long trunk laid lovingly across her throat, and its pretty head cuddled under the royal right ear.

When the princess had been good all through the week—for like all real live, nice children, she was sometimes naughty, but never bad—Nurse would allow her to ask her little friends to come on Wednesday morning early and spend the day, because Wednesday is the end of the week in that country.

Then, in the afternoon, when all the little dukes and duchesses and marquises and countesses had finished their rice pudding and had had their hands and faces washed after it, Nurse would say, ''Now, my dears, what would you like to do this afternoon?'' just as if she didn't know.

And the answer would be always the same: ''Oh, do let's go to the zoological gardens and ride on the big guinea pig and feed the rabbits and hear the dormouse asleep.''

So their pinafores were taken off and they all went to the zoological gardens, where twenty of them could ride at a time on the guinea pig, and where even the little ones could feed the great rabbits if some grown-up person were kind enough to lift them up for the purpose. And there always was some such person, because in Rotundia everybody was kind—except one.

Now that you have read as far as this you know, of course, that the kingdom of Rotundia was a very remarkable place, and if you are a thoughtful child—as of course you are—you will not need me to tell you what was the most remarkable thing about it. But in case you are not a thoughtful child—and it is just possible of course that you are *not*—I will tell you at once what that most remarkable thing was. *All the animals were the wrong sizes!* And this was how it happened.

In old, old, olden times, when all our world was just loose earth and air and fire and water mixed up anyhow like a pudding, and spinning round like mad trying to get the different things to settle into their proper places, a round piece of earth got loose and went spinning away by itself across the water which was just beginning to try to get spread out smooth into a real sea. And as the great round piece of earth flew away, going round and round as hard as it could, it met a long piece of hard rock that had got loose from another part of the puddingy mixture, and the rock was so hard, and was going so fast, that it ran its point through the round piece of earth and stuck out on the other side of it, so that the two together were like a very-very-much-too-big teetotum.[1]

---

[1] *A small top usually inscribed with letters, used in a game called put-and-take.*

I am afraid all this is very dull, but you know geography is never quite lively, and after all I must give you a little information even in a fairy tale—like the powder[1] in jam.

Well, when the pointed rock smashed into the round bit of earth the shock was so great that it set them spinning together through the air—which was just getting into its proper place, like all the rest of the things—only, as luck would have it, they forgot which way round they had been going, and began to spin round the wrong way. Presently Center of Gravity—a great giant who was managing the whole business—woke up in the middle of the earth and began to grumble.

"Hurry up," he said. "Come down and lie still, can't you?"

So the rock with the round piece of earth fell into the sea, and the point of the rock went into a hole that just fitted it in the stony sea bottom, and there it spun round the wrong way seven times and then lay still. And that round piece of land became, after millions of years, the Kingdom of Rotundia.

This is the end of the geography lesson. And now for just a little history, so that we may not feel that we are quite wasting our time. Of course, the consequence of the island having spun round the wrong way was that when the animals began to grow on the island they all grew the wrong sizes. The guinea pig, as you know, was as big as our elephants, and the elephant—dear little pet—was the size of the

[1] *Powdered sugar*

22

silly, tiny, black-and-tan dogs that ladies carry sometimes in their muffs. The rabbits were about the size of our rhinoceroses, and all about the wild parts of the island they had made their burrows as big as railway tunnels.

The dormouse, of course, was the biggest of all the creatures. I can't tell you how big he was. Even if you think of elephants it will not help you at all. Luckily there was only one of him, and he was always asleep. Otherwise I don't think the Rotundians could have borne with him. As it was, they made him a house, and it saved the expense of a brass band, because no band could possibly have been heard when the dormouse was talking in his sleep.

The men and women and children in this wonderful island were quite the right size, because their ancestors had come over with the Conqueror[1] long after the island had settled down and the animals grown on it.

Now the natural history lesson is over, and if you have been attending, you know more about Rotundia than anyone there did, except three people: the lord chief schoolmaster, and the princess's uncle—who was a magician, and knew everything without learning it—and Tom, the gardener's son.

Tom had learned more at school than anyone else, because he wished to take a prize. The prize offered by the lord chief schoolmaster was a *History of Rotundia,* beautifully bound, with the royal arms on the back. But after that day when the princess said she meant to marry Tom, the gardener's boy

[1] *William I*

thought it over, and he decided that the best prize in the world would be the princess, and this was the prize Tom meant to take. And when you are a gardener's son, and have decided to marry a princess, you will find that the more you learn at school the better.

The princess always played with Tom on the days when the little dukes and marquises did not come to tea—and when he told her he was almost sure of the first prize, she clapped her hands and said, "Dear Tom, dear good, clever Tom, you deserve all the prizes. And I will give you my pet elephant—and you can keep him till we're married."

The pet elephant was called Fido, and the gardener's son took him away in his coat pocket. He was the dearest little elephant you ever saw— about six inches long. But he was very, very wise— he could not have been wiser if he had been a mile high. He lay down comfortably in Tom's pocket, and when Tom put in his hand, Fido curled his little trunk round Tom's fingers with an affectionate confidence that made the boy's heart warm to his new little pet. What with the elephant, and the princess's affection, and the knowledge that the very next day he would receive the *History of Rotundia,* beautifully bound, with the royal arms on the cover, Tom could hardly sleep a wink. And besides, the dog did bark so terribly. There was only one dog in Rotundia—the kingdom could not afford to keep more than one: he was a Mexican lap dog of the kind that in most parts of the world only measures seven inches from the end of his dear nose to the tip of his darling tail—but in Rotundia he was bigger than I can possibly expect you to believe. And when he barked, his bark was so large that it filled up all the night and left no room for sleep or dreams or polite conversation, or anything else at all. He never barked at things that went on in the island—he was too large-minded for that—but when ships went blundering by in the dark, tumbling over the rocks at the end of the island, he would bark once or twice, just to let the ships know that they couldn't come playing about there just as they liked.

But on this particular night he barked, and barked, and barked—and the princess said, "Oh dear, oh dear, I wish he wouldn't, I am so sleepy." And Tom said to himself, "I wonder what ever is the matter. As soon as it's light I'll go and see."

So when it began to be pretty pink-and-yellow daylight, Tom got up and went out. And all the time the Mexican lap dog barked so that the houses shook, and the tiles on the roof of the palace rattled like milk cans in a cart whose horse is frisky.

"I'll go to the pillar," thought Tom, as he went through the town. The pillar, of course, was the top of the piece of rock that had stuck itself through Rotundia millions of years before, and made it spin round the wrong way. It was quite in the middle of the island, and stuck up ever so far, and when you were at the top you could see a great deal farther than when you were not.

As Tom went out from the town, and across the downs, he thought what a pretty sight it was to see the rabbits in the bright, dewy morning, frisking with their young ones by the mouths of their burrows. He did not go very near the rabbits, of course, because when a rabbit of that size is at play it does not always look where it is going, and it might easily have crushed Tom with its foot, and then it would have been very sorry afterwards. And Tom was a kind boy, and would not have liked to make even a rabbit unhappy. Earwigs in our country often get out of the way when they think you are going to walk on them. They too have kind hearts, and they would not like you to be sorry afterwards.

So Tom went on, looking at the rabbits and watching the morning grow more and more red and golden. And the Mexican lap dog barked all the time, till the church bells tinkled, and the chimney of the apple factory rocked again.

But when Tom got to the pillar, he saw that he would not need to climb to the top to find out what the dog was barking at.

For there, by the pillar, lay a very large purple dragon. His wings were like old purple umbrellas that have been very much rained on, and his head was large and bald, like the top of a purple toad-stool, and his tail, which was purple too, was very, very, very long, and thin, and tight like the lash of a carriage whip.

It was licking one of its purple umbrella-y wings, and every now and then it moaned and leaned its head back against the rocky pillar as though it felt faint. Tom saw at once what had happened. A flight of purple dragons must have crossed the island in the night, and this poor one must have knocked its wing and broken it against the pillar.

Everyone is kind to everyone in Rotundia, and Tom was not afraid of the dragon, although he had never spoken to one before. He had often watched them flying across the sea, but he had never expected to get to know one personally.

So now he said, "I am afraid you don't feel quite well."

The dragon shook his large purple head. He could not speak, but like all other animals, he could understand well enough when he liked.

"Can I get you anything?" asked Tom politely.

The dragon opened his purple eyes with an inquiring smile.

"A bun or two, now," said Tom coaxingly. "There's a beautiful bun tree quite close."

The dragon opened a great purple mouth and licked his purple lips, so Tom ran and shook the bun tree, and soon came back with an armful of fresh currant buns, and as he came he picked a few of the Bath[1] kind which grow on the low bushes near the pillar.

Because, of course, another consequence of the island's having spun the wrong way is that all the things we have to make—buns and cakes and shortbread—grow on trees and bushes, but in Rotundia they have to make their cauliflowers and cabbages and carrots and apples and onions, just as our cooks make puddings and turnovers.

Tom gave all the buns to the dragon, saying, "Here, try to eat a little. You'll soon feel better then."

The dragon ate up the buns, nodded rather ungraciously, and began to lick his wing again. So Tom left him and went back to the town with the news, and everyone was so excited at a real live dragon being on the island—a thing which had never happened before—that they all went out to

[1]Bath bun—a round bun made of sweet yeast dough containing eggs, butter, and currants and usually decorated with sugar, nuts, or pieces of candied fruit.

look at it, instead of going to the prizegiving, and the lord chief schoolmaster went with the rest. Now, he had Tom's prize, the *History of Rotundia,* in his pocket—the one bound in calf, with the royal arms on the cover—and it happened to drop out, and the dragon ate it, so Tom never got the prize after all. But the dragon, when he had got it, did not like it.

"Perhaps it's all for the best," said Tom. "I might not have liked that prize either, if I had got it."

It happened to be a Wednesday, so when the princess's friends were asked what they would like to do, all the little dukes and marquises and earls said, "Let's go and see the dragon." But the little duchesses and marchionesses and countesses said they were afraid.

Then Princess Mary Ann spoke up royally, and said, "Don't be silly, because it's only in fairy stories and histories of England, and things like that, that people are unkind and want to hurt each other. In Rotundia everyone is kind, and no one has anything to be afraid of, unless they're naughty; and then we know it's for our own good. Let's all go and see the dragon. We might take him some acid drops."

So they went. And all the titled children took it in turns to feed the dragon with acid drops, and he seemed pleased and flattered, and wagged as much of his purple tail as he could get at conveniently—for it was a very, very long tail indeed. But when it came to the princess's turn to give an acid drop to the dragon, he smiled a very wide smile and wagged his tail to the very last long inch of it, as much as to say, "Oh, you nice, kind, pretty little princess." But deep down in his wicked purple heart he was saying, "Oh, you nice, *fat*, pretty little princess, I should like to eat you instead of these silly acid drops." But of course nobody heard him except the princess's uncle, and he was a magician and accustomed to listening at doors. It was part of his trade.

Now, you will remember that I told you there was *one* wicked person in Rotundia, and I cannot conceal from you any longer that this Complete Bad was the princess's uncle James. Magicians are always bad, as you know from your fairy books, and some uncles are bad, as you see by the *Babes in the Wood*, or the *Norfolk Tragedy*, and one James at least was bad, as you have learned from your English history. And when anyone is a magician, and is also an uncle, and is named James as well, you need not expect anything nice from him. He is a Three Fold Complete Bad—and he will come to no good.

Uncle James had long wanted to get rid of the princess and have the kingdom to himself. He did not like many things—a nice kingdom was almost the only thing he cared for—but he had never seen his way quite clearly, because everyone is so kind in Rotundia that wicked spells will not work there, but run off those blameless islanders like water off a duck's back. Now, however, Uncle James thought there might be a chance for him—because he knew that now there were two wicked people on the island who could stand by each other—himself and the dragon. But he said nothing, only he exchanged a meaning glance with the dragon, and everyone went home to tea. And no one had seen the meaning glance, except Tom. And he went home, and told his elephant all about it. The intelligent little creature listened carefully, and then climbed from Tom's knee to the table, on which stood an ornamental calendar which the princess had given Tom for a Christmas present. With its tiny trunk the elephant pointed out a date—the fifteenth of August, the princess's birthday—and looked anxiously at its master.

"What is it, Fido—good little elephant—then?" said Tom, and the sagacious animal repeated its former gesture. Then Tom understood.

"Oh, something is to happen on her birthday? All right. I'll be on the lookout," and he was.

At first the people of Rotundia were quite pleased with the dragon, who lived by the pillar and fed himself from the bun trees, but by and by he began to wander. He would creep into the burrows made by the great rabbits, and excursionists, sporting on the downs, would see his long, tight, whiplike tail wriggling down a burrow and out of sight, and before they had time to say "There he goes," his ugly purple head would come poking out from another rabbit hole —perhaps just behind them—or laugh softly to itself just in their ears. And the dragon's laugh was not a merry one.

This sort of hide-and-seek amused people at first, but by and by it began to get on their nerves: and if you don't know what that means, ask Mother to tell you next time you are playing blindman's buff when she has a headache. Then the dragon got into the habit of cracking his tail, as people crack whips, and this also got on people's nerves. Then, too, little things began to be missed.

And you know how unpleasant that is, even in a private school, and in a public kingdom it is, of course, much worse. The things that were missed were nothing much at first—a few little elephants, a hippopotamus or two, and some giraffes, and things like that. It was nothing much, as I say, but it made people feel uncomfortable.

Then one day a favorite rabbit of the princess's called Frederick mysteriously disappeared, and then came a terrible morning when the Mexican lap dog was missing. He had barked ever since the dragon came to the island, and people had grown quite used to the noise. So when his barking suddenly ceased it woke everybody up—and they all went out to see what was the matter. And the lap dog was gone!

A boy was sent to wake the army, so that it might look for him. But the army was gone too! And now the people began to be frightened.

Then Uncle James came out on to the terrace of the palace, and he made the people a speech. He said, "Friends—fellow citizens—I cannot disguise from myself or from you that this purple dragon is a poor penniless exile, a helpless alien in our midst, and besides, he is a—is no end of a dragon."

The people thought of the dragon's tail and said, "Hear, hear."

Uncle James went on: "Something has happened to a gentle and defenseless member of our community. We don't know what has happened."

Everyone thought of the rabbit named Frederick, and groaned.

"The defenses of our country have been swallowed up," said Uncle James.

Everyone thought of the poor army.

"There is only one thing to be done." Uncle James was warming to his subject. "Could we ever forgive ourselves if by neglecting a simple precaution we lost more rabbits—or even, perhaps, our navy, our police, and our fire brigade? For I warn you that the purple dragon will respect nothing, however sacred."

Everyone thought of themselves—and they said, "What is the simple precaution?"

Then Uncle James said, "Tomorrow is the dragon's birthday. He is accustomed to have a present on his birthday. If he gets a nice present he will be in a hurry to take it away and show it to his friends, and he will fly off and never come back."

The crowd cheered wildly—and the princess from her balcony clapped her hands.

"The present the dragon expects," said Uncle James cheerfully, "is rather an expensive one. But when we give, it should not be in a grudging spirit, especially to visitors. What the dragon wants is a princess. We have only one princess, it is true, but far be it from us to display a miserly temper at such a moment. And the gift is worthless that costs the giver nothing. Your readiness to give up your princess will only show how generous you are."

The crowd began to cry, for they loved their princess, though they saw that their first duty was to be generous and give the poor dragon what it wanted.

The princess began to cry, for she did not want to be anybody's birthday present—especially a purple dragon's. And Tom began to cry because he was so angry.

He went straight home and told his little elephant, and the elephant cheered him up so much that presently the two grew quite absorbed in a teetotum which the elephant was spinning with his little trunk.

Early in the morning Tom went to the palace. He looked out across the downs—there were hardly any rabbits playing there now—and then he gathered white roses and threw them at the princess's window till she woke up and looked out.

"Come up and kiss me," she said.

So Tom climbed up the white rose bush and kissed the princess through the window, and said, "Many happy returns of the day."

Then Mary Ann began to cry, and said, "Oh, Tom—how can you? When you know quite well—"

"Oh, don't," said Tom. "Why, Mary Ann, my precious, my princess—what do you think I should be doing while the dragon was getting his birthday present? Don't cry, my own little Mary Ann! Fido and I have arranged everything. You've only got to do as you are told."

"Is that all?" said the princess. "Oh—that's easy—I've often done *that!*"

Then Tom told her what she was to do. And she kissed him again and again. "Oh, you dear, good, clever Tom," she said. "How glad I am that I gave you Fido. You two have saved me. You dears!"

The next morning Uncle James put on his best coat and hat and the waistcoat with the gold snakes on it—he was a magician, and he had a bright taste in waistcoats—and he called with a cab to take the princess out.

"Come, little birthday present," he said tenderly, "the dragon *will* be so pleased. And I'm glad to see you're not crying. You know, my child, we cannot begin too young to learn to think of the happiness of others rather than our own. I should not like my dear little niece to be selfish, or to wish to deny a trivial pleasure to a poor, sick dragon, far from his home and friends."

And the princess said she would try not to be selfish.

So presently the cab drew up near the pillar, and there was the dragon, his ugly purple head shining in the sun, and his ugly purple mouth half open.

Then Uncle James said, "Good morning, sir. We have brought you a small present for your birthday. We do not like to let such an anniversary go by without some suitable testimonial, especially to one who is a stranger in our midst. Our means are small, but our hearts are large. We have but one princess, but we give her freely—do we not, my child?"

The princess said she supposed so, and the dragon came a little nearer.

Suddenly a voice cried, "Run!" and there was Tom, and he had brought the zoological guinea pig and a pair of Belgian hares with him.

"Just to see fair," said Tom.

Uncle James was furious. "What do you mean, sir," he cried, "by intruding on a state function with your common rabbits and things? Go away, naughty little boy, and play with them somewhere else."

But while he was speaking the rabbits had come up one on each side of him, their great sides towering ever so high, and now they pressed him between them so that he was buried in their thick fur and almost choked. The princess, meantime, had run to the other side of the pillar and was peeping round it to see what was going on.

A crowd had followed the cab out of the town. Now they reached the scene of the "state function," and they all cried out, "Fair play—play fair! We can't go back on our word like this. Give a thing and take a thing? Why, it's *never* done. Let the poor exiled stranger dragon have his birthday present." And they tried to get at Tom—but the guinea pig stood in the way.

"Yes," Tom cried. "Fair play is a jewel. And your helpless exile shall have the princess—if he can catch her. Now then, Mary Ann."

Mary Ann looked round the big pillar and called to the dragon, "Bo! You can't catch me," and began to run as fast as ever she could, and the dragon after her. When the princess had run half a mile she stopped, dodged round a tree, and ran back to the pillar and round it, and the dragon after her. You see, he was so long he could not turn as quickly as she could.

Round and round the pillar ran the princess. The first time she ran round a long way from the pillar, and then nearer and nearer—with the dragon after her all the time, and he was so busy trying to catch her that he never noticed that Tom had tied the very end of his long, tight, whipcordy tail to the rock, so that the more the dragon ran round, the more times he twisted his tail round the pillar. It was exactly like winding a top—only the peg was the pillar, and the dragon's tail was the string. And the magician was safe between the

Belgian hares, and couldn't see anything but darkness, or do anything but choke.

When the dragon was wound on to the pillar, as much as he could possibly be, and as tight—like cotton on a reel—the princess stopped running, and though she had very little breath left, she managed to say "Yah—who's won now?"

This annoyed the dragon so much that he put out all his strength—spread his great purple wings, and tried to fly at her. Of course this pulled his tail, and pulled it very hard, so hard that as he pulled the tail *had* to come, and the pillar *had* to come round with the tail, and the island *had* to come round with the pillar, and in another minute the tail was loose, and the island was spinning round exactly like a teetotum. It spun so fast that everyone fell flat on their faces and held on tight to themselves, because they felt something was going to happen. All but the magician, who was choking between the Belgian hares, and felt nothing but fur and fury.

And something did happen. The dragon had sent the kingdom of Rotundia spinning the way it ought to have gone at the beginning of the world, and as it spun round all the animals began to change sizes. The guinea pigs got small and the elephants got big, and the men and women and children would have changed sizes, too, if they had not had the sense to hold on to themselves, very tight indeed, with both hands, which, of course, the animals could not be expected to know how to do. And the best of it was that when the small beasts got big and the big beasts got small the dragon got small too, and fell at the princess's feet —a little, crawling, purple newt with wings.

"Funny little thing," said the princess, when she saw it. "I will take it for a birthday present."

But while all the people were still on their faces, holding on tight to themselves, Uncle James, the magician, never thought of holding tight—he only thought of how to punish Belgian hares and the sons of gardeners. So when the big beasts grew small, he grew small with the other beasts, and the little purple dragon, when he fell at the princess's feet, saw there a very small magician named Uncle James. And the dragon took him because it wanted a birthday present.

So now all the animals were new sizes—and at first it seemed very strange to everyone to have great lumbering elephants and a tiny little dormouse, but they have got used to it now, and think no more of it than we do.

All this happened several years ago, and the other day I saw in *The Rotundia Times* an account of the wedding of the princess with Lord Thomas Gardener, K.C.D., and I knew she could not have married anyone but Tom, so I suppose they made him a lord on purpose for the wedding—and K.C.D., of course, means Clever Conqueror of the Dragon. If you think that is wrong it is only because you don't know how they spell in Rotundia. The paper said that among the beautiful presents of the bridegroom to the bride was an enormous elephant, on which the bridal pair made their wedding tour. This must have been Fido. You remember Tom promised to give him back to the princess when they were married. *The Rotundia Times* called the

37

married couple "the happy pair." It was clever of the paper to think of calling them that—it is such a pretty and novel expression, and I think it is truer than many of the things you see in papers.

Because, you see, the princess and the gardener's son were so fond of each other they could not help being happy—and besides, they had an elephant of their very own to ride on. If that is not enough to make people happy, I should like to know what is. Though, of course, I know there are some people who could not be happy unless they had a whale to sail on, and perhaps not even then. But they are greedy, grasping people, the kind who would take four helps of pudding, as likely as not, which neither Tom nor Mary Ann ever did.

Chapter 3

The Deliverers of Their Country

It all began with Effie's getting something in her
eye. It hurt very much indeed, and it felt
something like a red-hot spark—only it seemed
to have legs as well, and wings like a fly. Effie
rubbed and cried—not real crying, but the kind
your eye does all by itself without your being
miserable inside your mind—and then she went
to her father to have the thing in her eye taken
out.

Effie's father was a doctor, so of course he
knew how to take things out of eyes—he did it
very cleverly with a soft paintbrush dipped in
castor oil. When he had got the thing out, he
said, "This is very curious."

Effie had often got things in her eye before,
and her father had always seemed to think it was
natural—rather tiresome and naughty perhaps,
but still natural. He had never before thought it
curious. She stood holding her handkerchief to

her eye, and said, "I don't believe it's out."
People always say this when they have had
something in their eye.

"Oh, yes—it's *out*," said the doctor. "Here it
is on the brush. This is very interesting."

Effie had never heard her father say that about
anything that she had any share in. She said,
"*What?*"

The doctor carried the brush very carefully
across the room and held the point of it under his
microscope. Then he twisted the brass screws of
the microscope and looked through the top with
one eye.

"Dear me," he said. "Dear, *dear* me! Four
well-developed limbs, a long caudal appendage,
five toes, unequal in length. Almost like one of
the Lacertidae, yet there are traces of wings."
The creature under his eye wriggled a little in the
castor oil, and he went on: "Yes; a batlike wing.
A new specimen, undoubtedly. Effie, run round
to the professor and ask him to be kind enough to
step in for a few minutes."

"You might give me sixpence, Daddy," said
Effie, "because I did bring you the new
specimen. I took great care of it inside my eye,
and my eye *does* hurt."

The doctor was so pleased with the new
specimen that he gave Effie a shilling, and
presently the professor stepped round. He
stayed to lunch, and he and the doctor quarreled
very happily all the afternoon about the name
and the family of the thing that had come out of
Effie's eye.

But at teatime another thing happened.
Effie's brother Harry fished something out of his

tea, which he thought at first was an earwig. He was just getting ready to drop it on the floor, and end its life in the usual way, when it shook itself in the spoon—spread two wet wings, and flopped on to the tablecloth. There it sat stroking itself with its feet and stretching its wings, and Harry said, "Why, it's a tiny newt!"

The professor leaned forward before the doctor could say a word. "I'll give you a half a crown for it, Harry, my lad," he said, speaking very fast, and then he picked it up carefully on his handkerchief.

"It is a new specimen," he said, "and finer than yours, doctor."

It was a tiny lizard, about half an inch long—with scales and wings.

So now the doctor and the professor each had a specimen, and they were both very pleased. But before long these specimens began to seem less valuable. For the next morning, when the knife-boy was cleaning the doctor's boots, he suddenly dropped the brushes and the boot and the blacking, and screamed out that he was burned.

And from inside the boot came crawling a lizard as big as a kitten, with large, shiny wings.

"Why," said Effie, "I know what it is. It is a dragon like St. George killed."

And Effie was right. That afternoon Towser was bitten in the garden by a dragon about the size of a rabbit, which he had tried to chase, and next morning all the papers were full of the wonderful "winged lizards" that were appearing all over the country. The papers would not call them dragons, because, of course, no one believes in dragons nowadays—and at any rate the papers were not going to be so silly as to believe in fairy stories. At first there were only a few, but in a week or two the country was simply running alive with dragons of all sizes, and in the air you could sometimes see them as thick as a swarm of bees. They all looked alike except as to size. They were green with scales, and they had four legs and a long tail and great wings like bats' wings, only the wings were a pale, half-transparent yellow, like the gear cases on bicycles.

And they breathed fire and smoke, as all proper dragons must, but still the newspapers went on pretending they were lizards, until the editor of *The Standard* was picked up and carried away by a very large one, and then the other newspaper people had not anyone left to tell them what they ought not to believe. So that when the largest elephant in the zoo was carried off by a dragon, the papers gave up pretending—and put ALARMING PLAGUE OF DRAGONS at the top of the paper.

And you have no idea how alarming it was, and at the same time how aggravating. The large-sized dragons were terrible certainly, but when once you had found out that the dragons always went to bed early because they were afraid of the chill night air, you had only to stay indoors all day, and you were pretty safe from the big ones.

But the smaller sizes were a perfect nuisance. The ones as big as earwigs got in the soap, and they got in the butter. The ones as big as dogs got in the bath, and the fire and smoke inside them made them steam like anything when the cold water tap was turned on, so that careless people were often scalded quite severely. The ones that were as large as pigeons would get into workbaskets or corner drawers, and bite you when you were in a hurry to get a needle or a handkerchief.

The ones as big as sheep were easier to avoid, because you could see them coming, but when they flew in at the windows and curled up under your eiderdown, and you did not find them till you went to bed, it was always a shock. The ones this size did not eat people, only lettuces, but they always scorched the sheets and pillowcases dreadfully.

Of course the county council and the police did everything that could be done. It was no use offering the hand of the princess to anyone who killed a dragon. This way was all very well in olden times—when there was only one dragon and one princess, but now there were far more dragons than princesses—although the royal family was a large one. And besides, it would have been mere waste of princesses to offer rewards for killing dragons, because everybody killed as many dragons as they could quite out of their own heads and without rewards at all, just to get the nasty things out of the way. The county council undertook to cremate all dragons delivered at their offices between the hours of ten and two, and whole wagonloads and cartloads and truckloads of dead dragons could be seen any day of the week standing in a long line in the street where the county council lived. Boys brought barrowloads of dead dragons, and children on their way home from morning school would call in to leave the handful or two of little dragons they had brought in their satchels, or carried in their knotted pocket handkerchiefs. And yet there seemed to be as many dragons as ever. Then the police stuck up great wood and canvas towers covered with patent glue. When the dragons flew against these towers, they stuck fast, as flies and wasps do on the sticky papers in the kitchen, and when the towers were covered all over with dragons, the police inspector used to set light to the towers, and burned them and dragons and all.

And yet there seemed to be more dragons than ever. The shops were full of patent dragon poison and antidragon soap, and dragonproof curtains for the windows. And indeed, everything that could be done was done.

And yet there seemed to be more dragons than ever.

It was not very easy to know what would poison a dragon, because you see they ate such different things. The largest kind ate elephants as long as there were any, and then went on with horses and cows. Another size ate nothing but lilies of the valley, and a third size ate only prime ministers if they were to be had, and if not, would feed freely on boys in buttons. Another size lived on bricks, and three of them ate two thirds of the South Lambeth Infirmary in one afternoon.

But the size Effie was most afraid of was about as big as your dining room, and that size ate *little girls and boys*.

At first Effie and her brother were quite

pleased with the change in their lives. It was so amusing to sit up all night instead of going to sleep, and to play in the garden lighted by electric lamps.

And it sounded so funny to hear mother say, when they were going to bed, "Good night, my darlings, sleep sound all day, and don't get up too soon. You must not get up before it's *quite* dark. You wouldn't like the nasty dragons to catch you."

But after a time they got very tired of it all: they wanted to see the flowers and trees growing in the fields, and to see the pretty sunshine out of doors, and not just through glass windows and patent dragonproof curtains. And they wanted to play on the grass, which they were not allowed to do in the electric-lamp-lighted garden because of the night dew.

And they wanted so much to get out, just for once, in the beautiful, bright, dangerous daylight, that they began to try and think of some reason why they *ought* to go out. Only they did not like to disobey their mother.

But one morning their mother was busy preparing some new dragon poison to lay down in the cellars, and their father was bandaging the hand of the bootboy which had been scratched by one of the dragons who liked to eat prime ministers when they were to be had, so nobody remembered to say to the children "Don't get up till it is quite dark!"

"Go now," said Harry. "It would not be disobedient to go. And I know exactly what we ought to do, but I don't know how we ought to do it."

"What ought we to do?" said Effie.

"We ought to wake St. George, of course," said Harry. "He was the only person in his town who knew how to manage dragons—the people in the fairy tales don't count. But St. George is a real person, and he is only asleep, and he is waiting to be waked up. Only nobody believes in St. George now. I heard father say so."

"*We* do," said Effie.

"Of course we do. And don't you see, Ef, that's the very reason why we could wake him? You can't wake people if you don't believe in them, can you?"

Effie said no, but where could they find St. George?

"We must go and look," said Harry boldly. "You shall wear a dragonproof frock, made of stuff like the curtains. And I will smear myself all over with the best dragon poison, and—"

Effie clasped her hands and skipped with joy, and cried, "Oh, Harry! I know where we can find St. George! In St. George's Church, of course."

"Um," said Harry, wishing he had thought of it for himself, "you have a little sense sometimes, for a girl."

So next afternoon quite early, long before the beams of sunset announced the coming night, when everybody would be up and working, the two children got out of bed. Effie wrapped herself in a shawl of dragonproof muslin—there was no time to make the frock—and Harry made a horrid mess of himself with the patent dragon poison. It was warranted harmless to infants and invalids, so he felt quite safe.

Then they took hands and set out to walk to St. George's Church. As you know, there are many St. George's churches but fortunately they took the turning that leads to the right one, and went along in the bright sunlight, feeling very brave and adventurous.

There was no one about in the streets except dragons, and the place was simply swarming with them. Fortunately none of the dragons were just the right size for eating little boys and girls, or perhaps this story might have had to end here. There were dragons on the pavement, and dragons on the roadway, dragons basking on the front doorsteps of public buildings, and dragons preening their wings on the roofs in the hot afternoon sun. The town was quite green with them. Even when the children had got out of the town and were walking in the lanes, they noticed that the fields on each side were greener than usual with the scaly legs and tails, and some of the smaller sizes had made themselves asbestos nests in the flowering hawthorn hedges.

Effie held her brother's hand very tightly, and once when a fat dragon flopped against her ear she screamed out, and a whole flight of green dragons rose from the field at the sound, and sprawled away across the sky. The children could hear the rattle of their wings as they flew.

"Oh, I want to go home," said Effie.

"Don't be silly," said Harry. "Surely you haven't forgotten about the Seven Champions[1] and all the princes. People who are going to be

---

[1] *The patron saints of England, Scotland, Wales, Ireland, France, Italy, and Spain.*

their country's deliverers never scream and say they want to go home."

"And are we?" asked Effie. "Deliverers, I mean?"

"You'll see," said her brother, and on they went.

When they came to St. George's Church they found the door open, and they walked right in—but St. George was not there, so they walked round the churchyard outside, and presently they found the great stone tomb of St. George, with the figure of him carved in marble outside, in his armor and helmet, and with his hands folded on his breast.

"How ever can we wake him?" they said.

Then Harry spoke to St. George—but he would not answer. And he called, but St. George did not seem to hear. And then he actually tried to waken the great dragon slayer by shaking his marble shoulders. But St. George took no notice.

Then Effie began to cry, and she put her arms round St. George's neck as well as she could for the marble, which was very much in the way at the back, and she kissed the marble face, and she said, "Oh, dear, good, kind St. George, please wake up and help us."

And at that St. George opened his eyes sleepily, and stretched himself and said, "What's the matter, little girl?"

So the children told him all about it. He turned over in his marble and leaned on one elbow to listen. But when he heard that there were so many dragons he shook his head.

"It's no good," he said. "They would be one

too many for poor old George. You should have wakened me before. I was always for a fair fight —one man one dragon was my motto.''

Just then a flight of dragons passed overhead, and St. George half drew his sword.

But he shook his head again and pushed the sword back as the flight of dragons grew small in the distance.

"I can't do anything," he said. "Things have changed since my time. St. Andrew told me about it. They woke him up over the engineers' strike, and he came to talk to me. He says everything is done by machinery now. There must be some way of settling these dragons. By the way, what sort of weather have you been having lately?''

This seemed so careless and unkind that Harry could not answer, but Effie said, patiently, "It has been very fine. Father says it is the hottest weather there has ever been in this country.''

"Ah, I guessed as much," said the champion thoughtfully. "Well, the only thing would be... dragons can't stand wet and cold, that's the only thing. If you could find the taps.''

St. George was beginning to settle down again on his stone slab.

"Good night, very sorry I can't help you," he said, yawning behind his marble hand.

"Oh, but you can," cried Effie. "Tell us— what taps?''

"Oh, like in the bathroom," said St. George, still more sleepily. "And there's a looking glass, too. Shows you all the world and what's going on. St. Denis told me about it. Said it was a very pretty thing. I'm sorry I can't—good night.''

And he fell back into his marble and was fast asleep again in a moment.

"We shall never find the taps," said Harry. "I say, wouldn't it be awful if St. George woke up when there was a dragon near, the size that eats champions?"

Effie pulled off her dragonproof veil. "We didn't meet any the size of the dining room as we came along," she said. "I daresay we shall be quite safe."

So she covered St. George with the veil, and Harry rubbed off as much as he could of the dragon poison onto St. George's armor, so as to make everything quite safe for him.

"We might hide in the church till it is dark," he said, "and then—"

But at that moment a dark shadow fell on them, and they saw that it was a dragon exactly the size of the dining room at home.

So then they knew that all was lost. The dragon swooped down and caught the two children in his claws. He caught Effie by her green silk sash and Harry by the little point at the back of his Eton jacket—and then, spreading his great yellow wings, he rose into the air, rattling like a third-class carriage when the brake is hard on.

"Oh, Harry," said Effie, "I wonder when he will eat us!" The dragon was flying across woods and fields with great flaps of his wings that carried him a quarter of a mile at each flap.

Harry and Effie could see the country below, hedges and rivers and churches and farmhouses flowing away from under them, much faster than you see them running away from the sides of the fastest express train.

And still the dragon flew on. The children saw other dragons in the air as they went, but the dragon who was as big as the dining room never stopped to speak to any of them, but just flew on quite steadily.

"He knows where he wants to go," said Harry. "Oh, if he would only drop us before he gets there!"

But the dragon held on tight, and he flew and flew and flew until at last, when the children were quite giddy, he settled down, with a rattling of all his scales, on the top of a mountain. And he lay there on his great green scaly side, panting, and very much out of breath, because he had come such a long way. But his claws were fast in Effie's sash and the little point at the back of Harry's Eton jacket.

Then Effie took out the knife Harry had given her on her birthday. It only cost sixpence to begin with, and she had had it a month, and it never could sharpen anything but slate pencils, but somehow she managed to make that knife cut her sash in front, and crept out of it, leaving the dragon with only a green silk bow in one of his claws. That knife would never have cut Harry's jacket tail off, though, and when Effie had tried for some time she saw that this was so, and gave it up. But with her help Harry managed to wriggle quietly out of his sleeves, so that the dragon had only an Eton jacket in his other claw.

Then the children crept on tiptoe to a crack in the rocks and got in. It was much too narrow for the dragon to get in also, so they stayed in there and waited to make faces at the dragon when he felt rested enough to sit up and begin to think about eating them. He was very angry, indeed, when they made faces at him, and blew out fire and smoke at them but they ran farther into the cave so that he could not reach them, and when he was tired of blowing he went away.

But they were afraid to come out of the cave, so they went farther in and presently the cave opened out and grew bigger, and the floor was soft sand, and when they had come to the very end of the cave there was a door, and on it was written:

UNIVERSAL TAPROOM
PRIVATE
NO ONE ALLOWED INSIDE

So they opened the door at once just to peep in, and then they remembered what St. George had said.

"We can't be worse off than we are," said Harry, "with a dragon waiting for us outside. Let's go in."

So they went boldly into the taproom and shut the door behind them.

And now they were in a sort of room cut out of the solid rock, and all along one side of the room were taps, and all the taps were labeled with china labels like you see to baths. And as they could both read words of two syllables or even three sometimes, they understood at once that they had got to the place where the weather is turned on from.

There were six big taps labeled "Sunshine," "Wind," "Rain," "Snow," "Hail," "Ice," and a lot of little ones labeled "Fair to moderate," "Showery," "South breeze," "Nice growing weather for the crops," "Skating," "Good open weather," "South wind," "East wind," and so on.

And the big tap labeled "Sunshine" was turned full on. They could not see any sunshine—the cave was lighted by a skylight of blue glass—so they supposed the sunlight was pouring out by some other way, as it does with the tap that washes out the underneath parts of patent sinks in kitchens.

Then they saw that one side of the room was just a big looking glass, and when you looked in it you could see everything that was going on in the world—and all at once, too, which is not like most looking glasses. They saw the carts delivering the dead dragons at the county council offices, and they saw St. George asleep under the dragonproof veil. And they saw their mother at home crying because her children had gone out in the dreadful, dangerous daylight, and she was afraid a dragon had eaten them.

And they saw the whole of England, like a great puzzle map—green in the field parts and brown in the towns, and black in the places where they make coal, and crockery, and cutlery, and chemicals. And all over it, on the black parts, and on the brown, and on the green, there was a network of green dragons. And they could see that it was still broad daylight, and no dragons had gone to bed yet.

So Effie said, "Dragons do not like cold." And she tried to turn off the sunshine, but the tap was out of order, and that was why there had been so much hot weather, and why the dragons had been able to be hatched. So they left the sunshine tap alone, and they turned on the snow and left the tap full on while they went to look in the glass. There they saw the dragons running all sorts of ways like ants if you are cruel enough to pour water into an ant heap, which, of course, you never are. And the snow fell more and more.

Then Effie turned the rain tap quite full on, and presently the dragons began to wriggle less, and by and by some of them lay quite still, so the children knew the water had put out the fires inside them, and they were dead. So then they turned on the hail—only half on, for fear of breaking people's windows—and after a while there were no more dragons to be seen moving.

Then the children knew that they were indeed the deliverers of their country.

"They will put up a monument to us," said Harry, "as high as Nelson's! All the dragons are dead."

"I hope the one that was waiting outside for us is dead!" said Effie. "And about the monument, Harry, I'm not so sure. What can they do with such a lot of dead dragons? It would take years and years to bury them, and they could never be burned now they are so soaking wet. I wish the rain would wash them off into the sea."

But this did not happen, and the children began to feel that they had not been so frightfully clever after all.

"I wonder what this old thing's for," said Harry. He had found a rusty old tap, which seemed as though it had not been used for ages. Its china label was quite coated over with dirt and cobwebs. When Effie had cleaned it with a bit of her skirt—for curiously enough both the children had come out without pocket handkerchiefs—she found that the label said "Waste."

"Let's turn it on," she said. "It might carry off the dragons."

The tap was very stiff from not having been used for such a long time, but together they managed to turn it on, and then ran to the mirror to see what happened.

Already a great, round, black hole had opened in the very middle of the map of England, and the sides of the map were tilting themselves up, so that the rain ran down towards the hole.

"Oh, hurrah, hurrah, hurrah!" cried Effie, and she hurried back to the taps and turned on everything that seemed wet. "Showery," "Good open weather," "Nice growing weather for the crops," and even "South" and "Southwest," because she had heard her father say that those winds brought rain.

And now the floods of rain were pouring down on the country, and great sheets of water flowed towards the center of the map, and cataracts of water poured into the great round hole in the middle of the map, and the dragons were being washed away and disappearing down the waste-pipe in great green masses and scattered green shoals—single dragons and dragons by the dozen; of all sizes, from the ones that carry off elephants down to the ones that get in your tea.

And presently there was not a dragon left. So then they turned off the tap named "Waste," and they half-turned off the one labeled "Sunshine" —it was broken, so that they could not turn it off altogether—and they turned on "Fair to moderate" and "Showery" and both taps stuck, so that they could not be turned off, which accounts for our climate.

How did they get home again? By the Snowdon railway—of course.

*   *   *

And was the nation grateful? Well—the nation was very wet. And by the time the nation had got dry again it was interested in the new invention for toasting muffins by electricity, and all the dragons were almost forgotten. Dragons do not seem so important when they are dead and gone, and you know there never was a reward offered.

And what did father and mother say when Effie and Harry got home?

My dear, that is the sort of silly question you children always will ask. However, just for this once I don't mind telling you.

Mother said, "Oh, my darlings, my darlings, you're safe—you're safe! You naughty children—how could you be so disobedient? Go to bed at once!"

And their father the doctor said, "I wish I had known what you were going to do! I should have liked to preserve a specimen. I threw away the one I got out of Effie's eye. I intended to get a more perfect specimen. I did not anticipate this immediate extinction of the species."

The professor said nothing, but he rubbed his hands. He had kept his specimen—the one the size of an earwig that he gave Harry half a crown for—and he has it to this day.

You must get him to show it to you!

Chapter 4

**The Ice Dragon, or
Do as You Are Told**

This is the tale of the wonders that befell on the evening of the eleventh of December, when they did what they were told not to do. You may think that you know all the unpleasant things that could possibly happen to you if you are disobedient, but there are some things which even you do not know, and they did not know them either.

Their names were George and Jane.

There were no fireworks that year on Guy Fawkes Day, because the heir to the throne was not well. He was cutting his first tooth, and that is a very anxious time for any person—even for a royal one. He was really very poorly, so that fireworks would have been in the worst possible taste, even at Land's End or in the Isle of Man, while in Forest Hill, which was the home of Jane and George, anything of the kind was quite out of the question. Even the Crystal Palace, empty-headed as it is, felt that this was no time for Catherine wheels.

But when the prince had cut his tooth, rejoicings were not only admissible but correct, and the eleventh of December was proclaimed firework day. All the people were most anxious to show their loyalty, and to enjoy themselves at the same time. So there were fireworks, and torchlight processions, and set pieces at the Crystal Palace, with "Blessings on our Prince" and "Long Live Our Royal Darling" in different-colored fires. And the most private of boarding schools had a half-holiday. And even the children of plumbers and authors had tuppence each given them to spend as they liked.

George and Jane had sixpence each—and they spent the whole amount in a "golden rain," which would not light for ever so long, and when it did light, went out almost at once, so they had to look at the fireworks in the gardens next door, and at the ones at the Crystal Palace, which were very glorious indeed.

All their relations had colds in their heads, so Jane and George were allowed to go out into the garden alone to let off their firework. Jane had put on her fur cape and her thick gloves, and her hood with the silver-fox fur on it which was made out of mother's old muff. And George had his overcoat with the three capes, and his comforter, and father's sealskin traveling cap with the pieces that come down over your ears.

It was dark in the garden, but the fireworks all about made it seem very gay, and though the children were cold they were quite sure that they were enjoying themselves.

They got up on the fence at the end of the garden to see better, and then they saw, very far away, where the edge of the dark world is, a shining line of straight, beautiful lights arranged in a row, as if they were the spears carried by a fairy army.

"Oh, how pretty," said Jane. "I wonder what they are. It looks as if the fairies were planting little shining baby poplar trees, and watering them with liquid light."

"Liquid fiddlestick!" said George. He had been to school, so he knew that these were only the aurora borealis, or northern lights. And he said so.

"But what *is* the rory bory what's-its-name?" asked Jane. "Who lights it, and what's it there for?"

George had to own that he had not learned that.

"But I know," said he, "that it has something to do with the Great Bear, and the Dipper, and the Plough, and Charles's Wain.[1]"

"And what are they?" asked Jane.

"Oh, they're the surnames of some of the star families. There goes a jolly rocket," answered George, and Jane felt as if she almost understood about the star families.

The fairy spears of light twinkled and gleamed: they were much prettier than the big, blaring, blazing bonfire that was smoking and flaming and spluttering in the next-door-but-one garden —prettier even than the colored fires at the Crystal Palace.

"I wish we could see them nearer," Jane said. "I wonder if the star families are nice

[1]*Different names of the same constellation, Ursa Major.*

families—the kind that mother would like us to go to tea with, if we were little stars?''

"They aren't that sort of families at all, silly," said her brother, kindly trying to explain. "I only said 'families' because a kid like you wouldn't have understood if I'd said constel—. And besides, I've forgotten the end of the word. Anyway, the stars are all up in the sky, so you can't go to tea with them."

"No," said Jane. "I said if we were little stars."

"But we aren't," said George.

"No," said Jane with a sigh. "I know that. I'm not so stupid as you think, George. But the Tory bories are somewhere at the edge. Couldn't we go and see *them*?"

"Considering you're eight, you haven't much sense." George kicked his boots against the paling to warm his toes. "It's half the world away."

"It looks very near," said Jane, hunching up her shoulders to keep her neck warm.

"They're close to the north pole," said George. "Look here—I don't care a straw about the aurora borealis, but I shouldn't mind discovering the north pole: it's awfully difficult and dangerous, and then you come home and write a book about it with a lot of pictures, and everybody says how brave you are."

Jane got off the fence.

"Oh, George, *let's*," she said. "We shall never have such a chance again—all alone by ourselves —and quite late too."

"I'd go right enough if it wasn't for you," George answered gloomily, "but you know they always say I lead you into mischief—and if we went to the north pole we should get our boots wet, as likely as not, and you remember what they said about not going on the grass.''

"They said the *lawn*," said Jane. "We're not going on the *lawn*. Oh, George, do, *do* let's. It doesn't look so *very* far—we could be back before they had time to get dreadfully angry."

"All right," said George, "but mind *I* don't want to go."

So off they went. They got over the fence, which was very cold and white and shiny because it was beginning to freeze, and on the other side of the fence was somebody else's garden, so they got out of that as quickly as they could, and beyond that was a field where there was another big bonfire, with people standing round it who looked quite black.

"It's like Indians," said George, and wanted to stop and look, but Jane pulled him on, and they passed by the bonfire and got through a gap in the hedge into another field—a dark one. And far away, beyond quite a number of other dark fields, the northern lights shone and sparkled and twinkled.

Now, during the winter the arctic regions come much farther south than they are marked on the map. Very few people know this, though you would think they could tell it by the ice in the jugs of a morning. And just when George and Jane were starting for the north pole, the arctic regions had come down very nearly as far as Forest Hill, so that, as the children walked on, it grew colder and colder, and presently they saw that the fields were covered with snow, and there were great icicles hanging from all the hedges and gates. And the northern lights still seemed some way off.

They were crossing a very rough, snowy field when Jane first noticed the animals. There were white rabbits and white hares, and all sorts and sizes of white birds, and some larger creatures in the shadows of the hedges which Jane was sure were wolves and bears.

"Polar bears and arctic wolves, of course I mean," she said, for she did not want George to think her stupid again.

There was a great hedge at the end of this field, all covered with snow and icicles, but the children found a place where there was a hole, and as no bears or wolves seemed to be just in that part of the hedge, they crept through and scrambled out of the frozen ditch on the other side. And then they stood still and held their breath with wonder.

For in front of them, running straight and smooth right away to the northern lights, lay a great wide road of pure dark ice, and on each side were tall trees all sparkling with white frost, and from the boughs of the trees hung strings of stars threaded on fine moonbeams, and shining so brightly that it was like a beautiful fairy daylight. Jane said so, but George said it was like the electric lights at the Earl's Court Exhibition.

The rows of trees went as straight as ruled lines away—away and away—and at the other end of them shone the aurora borealis.

There was a signpost—of silvery snow—and on it in letters of pure ice the children read:

THIS WAY TO THE NORTH POLE

Then George said, "Way or no way, I know a slide when I see one—so here goes." And he took a run on the frozen snow, and Jane took a run when she saw him do it, and the next moment they were sliding away, each with feet half a yard apart, along the great slide that leads to the north pole.

This great slide is made for the convenience of the polar bears, who, during the winter months, get their food from the army and navy stores—and it is the most perfect slide in the world. If you have never come across it, it is because you have never let off fireworks on the eleventh of December, and have never been thoroughly naughty and disobedient. But do not be these things in the hope of finding the great slide—because you might find something quite different, and then you would be sorry.

The great slide is like common slides in this, that when once you have started you have to go on to the end—unless you fall down—and then it hurts just as much as the smaller kind on ponds. The great slide runs downhill all the way, so that you keep on going faster and faster and faster. George and Jane went so fast that they had no time to notice the scenery.

They only saw the long lines of frosted trees and the starry lamps, and—on each side, rushing back as they slid on—a very broad, white world and a very large, black night. And overhead, as well as in the trees, the stars were bright like silver lamps, and far ahead shone and trembled and sparkled the line of fairy spears. Jane said that, and George said, "I can see the northern lights quite plain."

It is very pleasant to slide and slide and slide on clear, dark ice—especially if you feel you are really going somewhere, and more especially if that somewhere is the north pole. The children's feet made no noise on the ice, and they went on and on in a beautiful white silence.

But suddenly the silence was shattered and a cry rang out over the snow: "Hi! You there! Stop!"

"Tumble for your life!" cried George, and he fell down at once, because it is the only way to stop. Jane fell on top of him—and then they crawled on hands and knees to the snow at the edge of the slide—and there was a sportsman, dressed in a peaked cap and a frozen moustache, like the one you see in the pictures about Ice Peter, and he had a gun in his hand.

"You don't happen to have any bullets about you?" said he.

"No," George said, truthfully. "I had five of father's revolver cartridges, but they were taken away the day Nurse turned out my pockets to see if I had taken the knob of the bathroom door by mistake."

"Quite so," said the sportsman. "These accidents will occur. You don't carry firearms, then, I presume?"

"I haven't any fire*arms*," said George, "but I have a fire*work*. It's only a squib one of the boys gave me, if that's any good," and he began to feel among the string, and peppermints, and buttons, and tops, and nibs, and chalk, and postage stamps in his pockets.

"One could but try," the sportsman replied, and he held out his hand.

But Jane pulled at her brother's jacket tail and whispered, "Ask him what he wants it for."

So then the sportsman had to confess that he wanted the firework to kill the white grouse with. And when they came to look, there was the white grouse himself, sitting in the snow, looking quite pale and careworn, and waiting anxiously for the matter to be decided one way or the other.

George put all the things back in his pockets and said, "No, I couldn't. The season for shooting him stopped yesterday—I heard father say so—so it wouldn't be fair, anyhow. I'm very sorry, but I can't—so there!"

The sportsman said nothing, only he shook his fist at Jane, and then he got on the slide and tried to go towards the Crystal Palace—which was not easy, because that way is uphill. So they left him trying, and went on.

Before they started, the white grouse thanked them in a few pleasant, well-chosen words, and then they took a sideway slanting run and started off again on the great slide, and so away towards the north pole and the twinkling, beautiful lights.

The great slide went on and on, and the lights did not seem to come much nearer, and the white silence wrapped them round as they slid along the wide, icy path.

Then once again the silence was broken to bits by someone calling "Hi! You there! Stop!"

"Tumble for your life!" cried George, and tumbled as before, stopping in the only possible way, and Jane stopped on top of him, and they crawled to the edge, and came suddenly on the butterfly collector who was looking for specimens with a pair of blue glasses, and a blue net, and a blue book with colored plates.

"Excuse me," said the collector, "but have you such a thing as a needle about you—a very long needle?"

"I have a needle *book*," replied Jane politely,

"but there aren't any needles in it now. George took them all to do the things with pieces of cork—in the *Boy's Own Scientific Experimenter* and *The Young Mechanic*. He did not do the things, but he did for the needles."

"Curiously enough," said the collector, "I, too, wished to use the needle in connection with cork."

"I have a hatpin in my hood," said Jane. "I fastened the fur with it when it caught in the nail on the greenhouse door. It is very long and sharp—would that do?"

"One could but try," said the collector, and Jane began to feel for the pin. But George pinched her arm and whispered, "Ask what he wants it for." Then the collector had to own that he wanted the pin to stick through the great arctic moth. "A magnificent specimen," he added, "which I am most anxious to preserve."

And there, sure enough, in the collector's butterfly net sat the great arctic moth listening attentively to the conversation.

"Oh, I couldn't!" cried Jane. And while George was explaining to the collector that they would really rather not, Jane opened the blue folds of the butterfly net and asked the moth, quietly, if it would please step outside for a moment. And it did.

When the collector saw that the moth was free, he seemed less angry than grieved. "Well, well," said he, "here's a whole arctic expedition thrown away! I shall have to go home and fit out another. And that means a lot of writing to the papers and things. You seem to be a singularly thoughtless little girl."

So they went on, leaving him, too, trying to go uphill towards the Crystal Palace.

When the great white arctic moth had returned thanks in a suitable speech, George and Jane took a sideways slanting run and started sliding again, between the star lamps along the great slide, towards the north pole. They went faster and faster, and the lights ahead grew brighter and brighter—so that they could not keep their eyes open, but had to blink and wink as they went—and then suddenly the great slide ended in an immense heap of snow, and George and Jane shot right into it because they could not stop themselves, and the snow was soft so that they went in up to their very ears.

When they had picked themselves out, and thumped each other on the back to get rid of the snow, they shaded their eyes and looked, and there, right in front of them, was the wonder of wonders—the north pole—towering high and white and glistening, like an ice lighthouse, and it was quite, quite close, so that you had to put your head as far back as it would go, and farther, before you could see the high top of it. It was made entirely of ice. You will hear grown-up people talk a great deal of nonsense about the north pole, and when you are grown-up, it is even possible that you may talk nonsense about it yourself (the most unlikely things do happen), but deep down in your heart you must always remember that the north pole is made of clear ice, and could not possibly, if you come to think of it, be made of anything else.

All round the pole, making a bright ring about it, were hundreds of little fires, and the flames of them did not flicker and twist, but went up blue and green and rosy and straight like the stalks of dream lilies.

Jane said so, but George said they were as straight as ramrods.

And these flames were the aurora borealis—which the children had seen as far away as Forest Hill.

The ground was quite flat, and covered with smooth, hard snow, which shone and sparkled like the top of a birthday cake which has been iced at home. The ones done at the shops do not shine and sparkle, because they mix flour with the icing sugar.

"It is like a dream," said Jane.

And George said, "It *is* the north pole. Just think of the fuss people always make about getting here—and it was no trouble at all, really."

"I daresay lots of people have *got* here," said Jane, dismally. "It's not the getting *here*—I see that—it's the getting back again. Perhaps no one will ever know that *we* have been here, and the robins will cover us with leaves and—"

"Nonsense," said George. "There aren't any robins, and there aren't any leaves. It's just the north pole, that's all, and I've found it. And now I shall try to climb up and plant the British flag on the top—my handkerchief will do—and if it really *is* the north pole, my pocket compass Uncle James gave me will spin round and round, and then I shall know. Come on."

So Jane went on. And when they got close to the clear, tall, beautiful flames they saw that there was a great, queer-shaped lump of ice all round the bottom of the pole—clear, smooth, shining ice, that was deep, beautiful Prussian blue, like icebergs, in the thick parts, and all sorts of wonderful, glimmery, shimmery, changing colors in the thin parts, like the cut-glass chandelier in Grandma's house in London.

"It's a very curious shape," said Jane. "It's almost like"—she drew back a step to get a better view of it—"it's almost like a *dragon*."

"It's much more like the lampposts on the Thames embankment," said George, who had noticed a curly thing like a tail that went twisting up the north pole.

"Oh, George," cried Jane, "it *is* a dragon. I can see its wings. Whatever shall we do?"

And, sure enough, it *was* a dragon—a great, shining, winged, scaly, clawy, big-mouthed dragon—made of pure ice. It must have gone to sleep curled round the hole where the warm steam used to come up from the middle of the earth. And then when the earth got colder, and the column of steam froze and was turned into the north pole, the dragon must have got frozen in his sleep—frozen too hard to move—and there he stayed. And though he was very terrible, he was very beautiful too.

Jane said so, but George said, "Oh, don't bother. I'm thinking how to get on to the pole and try the compass without waking the brute."

The dragon certainly was beautiful, with his deep, clear Prussian-blueness and his rainbow-colored glitter. And rising from within the cold coil of the frozen dragon the north pole shot up like a pillar made of one great diamond, and every now and then it cracked a little, from sheer coldness. The sound of the cracking was the only thing that broke the great white silence in the midst of which the dragon lay like an enormous jewel, and the straight flames went up all round him like the stalks of tall lilies.

And as the children stood there looking at the most wonderful sight their eyes had ever seen, there was a soft padding of feet and a hurry-scurry behind them, and from the outside darkness beyond the flame stalks came a crowd of little brown creatures running, jumping, scrambling, tumbling head over heels, and on all fours, and some even walking on their heads. They caught hands as they came near the fires, and danced round in a ring.

"It's bears," said Jane. "I know it is. Oh, how I wish we hadn't come. And my boots are so wet."

The dancing ring broke up suddenly, and the next moment hundreds of furry arms clutched at George and Jane, and they found themselves in the middle of a great, soft, heaving crowd of little fat people in brown fur dresses, and the white silence was quite gone.

"Bears, indeed," cried a shrill voice. "You'll wish we *were* bears before you've done with us."

This sounded so dreadful that Jane began to cry. Up to now the children had only seen the most beautiful and wondrous things, but now they began to be sorry they had done what they were told not to, and the difference between "lawn" and "grass" did not seem so great as it had done at Forest Hill.

Directly Jane began to cry, all the brown people started back. No one cries in the arctic regions for fear of being struck so by the frost. So that these people had never seen anyone cry before.

"Don't cry *really*," whispered George, "or you'll get chilblains in your eyes. But *pretend* to howl—it frightens them."

So Jane went on pretending to howl, and the real crying stopped: it always does when you begin to pretend. You try it.

Then, speaking very loud so as to be heard over the howls of Jane, George said, "Yah—who's afraid? We are George and Jane—who are you?"

"We are the sealskin dwarfs," said the brown people, twisting their furry bodies in and out of the crowd like the changing glass in kaleidoscopes. "We are very precious and expensive, for we are made, throughout, of the very best sealskin."

"And what are those fires for?" bellowed George—for Jane was crying louder and louder.

"Those," shouted the dwarfs, coming a step nearer, "are the fires we make to thaw the dragon. He is frozen now—so he sleeps curled up round the pole—but when we have thawed him with our fires he will wake up and go and eat everybody in the world except us."

"Whatever—do—you—want—him—to—do—that—for?" yelled George.

"Oh—just for spite," bawled the dwarfs, carelessly—as if they were saying "Just for fun."

Jane left off crying to say, "You *are* heartless."

"No, we aren't," they said. "Our hearts are made of the finest sealskin, just like little fat sealskin purses."

And they all came a step nearer. They were very fat and round. Their bodies were like sealskin jackets on a very stout person, their heads were like sealskin muffs, their legs were like sealskin boas, and their hands and feet were like sealskin tobacco pouches. And their faces were like seals' faces, inasmuch as they, too, were covered with sealskin.

"Thank you so much for telling us," said George. "Good evening. (Keep on howling, Jane!)"

But the dwarfs came a step nearer, muttering and whispering. Then the muttering stopped—and there was a silence so deep that Jane was afraid to howl in it. But it was a brown silence, and she had liked the white silence better.

Then the chief dwarf came quite close and said, "What's that on your head?"

And George felt it was all up—for he knew it was his father's sealskin cap.

The dwarf did not wait for an answer. "It's made of one of *us*," he screamed, "or else one of the seals, our poor relations. Boy, now your fate is sealed!"

And looking at the wicked seal faces all around them, George and Jane felt that their fate was sealed indeed.

The dwarfs seized the children in their furry arms. George kicked, but it is no use kicking sealskin, and Jane howled, but the dwarfs were getting used to that. They climbed up the dragon's side and dumped the children down on his icy spine, with their backs against the north pole. You have no idea how cold it was—the kind of cold that makes you feel small and prickly inside your clothes, and makes you wish you had twenty times as many clothes to feel small and prickly inside of.

The sealskin dwarfs tied George and Jane to the north pole, and as they had no ropes, they bound them with snow wreaths, which are very strong when they are made in the proper way, and they heaped up the fires very close and said, "Now the dragon will get warm, and when he gets warm he will wake and when he wakes he will be hungry, and when he is hungry he will eat, and the first thing he will eat will be *you.*"

The little, sharp, many-colored flames sprang up like the stalks of dream lilies, but no heat came to the children, and they grew colder and colder.

"We won't be very nice when the dragon does eat us, that's one comfort," said George. "We shall be turned into ice long before that."

Suddenly there was a flapping of wings, and the white grouse perched on the dragon's head and said, "Can I be of any assistance?"

Now, by this time the children were so cold, so cold, so very, very cold, that they had forgotten everything but that, and they could say nothing else.

So the white grouse said, "One moment. I am only too grateful for opportunity of showing my sense of your manly conduct about the firework!"

And the next moment there was a soft whispering rustle of wings overhead, and then, fluttering slowly, softly down, came hundreds and thousands of little white fluffy feathers. They fell on George and Jane like snowflakes, and like flakes of fallen snow lying one above another, they grew into a thicker and thicker covering, so that presently the children were buried under a heap of white feathers, and only their faces peeped out.

"Oh, you dear, good, kind white grouse," said Jane. "But you'll be cold yourself, won't you, now you have given us all your pretty dear feathers?"

The white grouse laughed, and his laugh was echoed by thousands of kind, soft bird voices.

"Did you think all those feathers came out of one breast? There are hundreds and hundreds of us here, and every one of us can spare a little tuft of soft breast feathers to help to keep two kind little hearts warm!"

Thus spoke the grouse, who certainly had very pretty manners.

So now the children snuggled under the feathers and were warm, and when the sealskin dwarfs tried to take the feathers away, the grouse and his friends flew in their faces with flappings and screams, and drove the dwarfs back. They are a cowardly folk.

The dragon had not moved yet—but then he might at any moment get warm enough to move, and though George and Jane were now warm, they were not comfortable nor easy in their minds.

They tried to explain to the grouse, but though he is polite, he is not clever, and he only said, "You've got a warm nest, and we'll see that no one takes it from you. What more can you possibly want?"

Just then came a new, strange, jerky fluttering of wings far softer than the grouse's, and George and Jane cried out together, "Oh, *do* mind your wings in the fires!"

For they saw at once that it was the great white arctic moth.

74

"What's the matter?" he asked, settling on the dragon's tail.

So they told him.

"Sealskin, are they?" said the moth. "Just you wait a minute!"

He flew off very crookedly, dodging the flames, and presently he came back, and there were so many moths with him that it was as if a live sheet of white wingedness were suddenly drawn between the children and the stars.

And then the doom of the bad sealskin dwarfs fell suddenly on them.

For the great sheet of winged whiteness broke up and fell, as snow falls, and it fell upon the sealskin dwarfs. And every snowflake of it was a live, fluttering, hungry moth, that buried its greedy nose deep in the sealskin fur.

Grown-up people will tell you that it is not moths but moths' children who eat fur—but this is only when they are trying to deceive you. When they are not thinking about you they say, "I fear the moths have got at my ermine tippet," or, "Your poor Aunt Emma had a lovely sable cloak, but it was eaten by moths." And now there were more moths than have ever been together in this world before, all settling on the sealskin dwarfs.

The dwarfs did not see their danger till it was too late. Then they called for camphor and bitter apple, and oil of lavender, and yellow soap and borax, and some of the dwarfs even started to get these things, but long before any of them could get to the chemist's all was over. The moths ate, and ate, and ate, till the sealskin dwarfs, being sealskin throughout, even to the empty hearts of them, were eaten down to the very life—and they fell one by one on the snow and so came to their end. And all round the north pole the snow was brown with their flat bare pelts.

"Oh, thank you—thank you, darling arctic moth," cried Jane. "You *are* good—I do hope you haven't eaten enough to disagree with you afterwards!"

Millions of moth voices answered, with laughter as soft as moth wings, "We should be a poor set of fellows if we couldn't overeat ourselves for once in a way—to oblige a friend."

And off they all fluttered, and the white grouse flew off, and the sealskin dwarfs were all dead, and the fires went out, and George and Jane were left alone in the dark with the dragon!

"Oh, dear," said Jane, "this is the worst of all!"

"We've no friends left to help us," said George. He never thought that the dragon himself might help them—but then that was an idea that would never have occurred to any boy.

It grew colder and colder and colder, and even under the grouse feathers the children shivered.

Then, when it was so cold that it could not manage to be any colder without breaking the thermometer, it stopped. And then the dragon uncurled himself from round the north pole, and stretched his long, icy length over the snow, and said, "This is something like! How faint those fires did make me feel!"

The fact was, the sealskin dwarfs had gone the wrong way to work: the dragon had been frozen so long that now he was nothing but solid ice all through, and the fires only made him feel as if he were going to die.

But when the fires were out he felt quite well, and

very hungry. He looked round for something to eat. But he never noticed George and Jane, because they were frozen to his back.

He moved slowly off, and the snow wreaths that bound the children to the pole gave way with a snap, and there was the dragon, crawling south—with Jane and George on his great, scaly, icy shining back. Of course the dragon had to go south if he went anywhere, because when you get to the north pole there is no other way to go. The dragon rattled and tinkled as he went, exactly like the cut-glass chandelier when you touch it, as you are strictly forbidden to do. Of course there are a million ways of going south from the north pole— so you will own that it was lucky for George and Jane when the dragon took the right way and suddenly got his heavy feet on the great slide. Off he went, full speed, between the starry lamps, towards Forest Hill and the Crystal Palace.

"He's going to take us home," said Jane. "Oh, he is a good dragon. I *am* glad!"

And George was rather glad, too, though neither of the children felt at all sure of their welcome, especially as their feet were wet, and they were bringing a strange dragon home with them.

They went very fast, because dragons can go uphill as easily as down. You would not understand why if I told you—because you are only in long division at present; yet if you want me to tell you, so that you can show off to other boys, I will. It is because dragons can get their tails into the fourth dimension and hold on there, and when you can do that everything else is easy.

The dragon went very fast, only stopping to eat the collector and the sportsman, who were still struggling to go up the slide—vainly, because they had no tails, and had never even heard of the fourth dimension.

And when the dragon got to the end of the slide he crawled very slowly across the dark field beyond the field where there was a bonfire, next to the next-door garden at Forest Hill. He went slower and slower, and in the bonfire field he stopped altogether, and because the arctic regions had not got down so far as that, and because the bonfire was very hot, the dragon began to melt, and melt, and melt—and before the children knew what he was doing they found themselves sitting in a large pool of water, and their boots were as wet as wet, and there was not a bit of dragon left!

So they went indoors.

Of course some grown-up or other noticed at once that the boots of George and of Jane were wet and muddy, and that they had both been sitting down in a very damp place, so they were sent to bed immediately.

It was long past their time, anyhow.

Now, if you are of an inquiring mind—not at all a nice thing in a little boy who reads fairy tales—you will want to know how it is that since the sealskin dwarfs have all been killed, and the fires all been let out, the aurora borealis shines, on cold nights, as brightly as ever.

My dear, I do not know! I am not too proud to own that there are some things I know nothing about—and this is one of them. But I do know that whoever has lighted those fires again, it is certainly not the sealskin dwarfs. They were all eaten by moths—and moth-eaten things are of no use, even to light fires!

Chapter 5

The Island of the Nine Whirlpools

The dark arch that led to the witch's cave was hung round with a black and yellow fringe of live snakes. As the queen went in, keeping carefully in the middle of the arch, all the snakes lifted their wicked, flat heads and stared at her with their wicked, yellow eyes. You know it is not manners to stare, even at royalty, except of course for cats. And the snakes had been so badly brought up that they even put their tongues out at the poor lady. Nasty, thin, sharp tongues they were too.

Now, the queen's husband was, of course, the king. And besides being a king he was an enchanter, and considered to be quite at the top of his profession, so he was very wise, and he knew that when kings and queens want children, the queen always goes to see a witch. So he gave the queen the witch's address, and the queen called on her, though she was very frightened and did not like it at all. The witch was sitting by a fire of sticks, stirring something bubbly in a shiny copper cauldron.

"What do *you* want, my dear?" she said to the queen.

"Oh, if you please," said the queen, "I want a baby—a very nice one. We don't want any expense spared. My husband said—"

"Oh, yes," said the witch. "I know all about *him*. And so you want a child? Do you know it will bring you sorrow?"

"It will bring me joy first," said the queen.

"Great sorrow," said the witch.

"Greater joy," said the queen.

Then the witch said, "Well, have your own way. I suppose it's as much as your place is worth to go back without it?"

"The king would be very much annoyed," said the poor queen.

"Well, well," said the witch. "What will you give me for the child?"

"Anything you ask for, and all I have," said the queen.

"Then give me your gold crown."

The queen took it off quickly.

"And your necklace of blue sapphires."

The queen unfastened it.

"And your pearl bracelets."

The queen unclasped them.

"And your ruby clasps."

And the queen undid the clasps.

"Now the lilies from your breast."

The queen gathered together the lilies.

"And the diamonds of your little bright shoe buckles."

The queen pulled off her shoes.

Then the witch stirred the stuff that was in the cauldron, and one by one, she threw in the gold crown, and the sapphire necklace, and the pearl bracelets, and the ruby clasps, and the diamonds of the little bright shoe buckles, and last of all, she threw in the lilies.

And the stuff in the cauldron boiled up in foaming flashes of yellow, and blue, and red, and white, and silver, and sent out a sweet scent, and presently the witch poured it out into a pipkin and set it to cool in the doorway among the snakes.

Then she said to the queen, "Your child will have hair as golden as your crown, eyes as blue as your sapphires. The red of your rubies will lie on its lips, and its skin will be clear and pale as your pearls. Its soul will be white and sweet as your lilies, and your diamonds will be no clearer than its wits."

"Oh, thank you, thank you," said the queen, "and when will it come?"

"You will find it when you get home."

"And won't you have something for yourself?" asked the queen. "Any little thing you fancy—would you like a country, or a sack of jewels?"

"Nothing, thank you," said the witch. "I could make more diamonds in a day than I should wear in a year."

"Well, but do let me do some little thing for you," the queen went on. "Aren't you tired of being a witch? Wouldn't you like to be a duchess or a princess, or something like that?"

"There is one thing I should rather like," said the witch, "but it's hard to get in my trade."

"Oh, tell me what," said the queen.

"I should like someone to love me," said the witch.

Then the queen threw her arms round the witch's neck and kissed her half a hundred times. "Why," she said, "I love you better than my life! You've given me the baby—and the baby shall love you too."

"Perhaps it will," said the witch, "and when the sorrow comes send for me. Each of your fifty kisses will be a spell to bring me to you. Now, drink up your medicine, there's a dear, and run along home."

So the queen drank the stuff in the pipkin, which was quite cool by this time, and she went out under the fringe of snakes, and they all behaved like good Sunday-school children. Some of them even tried to drop a curtsy to her as she went by, though that is not easy when you are hanging wrong way up by your tail. But the snakes knew the queen was friends with their mistress, so of course they had to do their best to be civil.

When the queen got home, sure enough there was the baby lying in the cradle, with the royal arms blazoned on it, crying as naturally as possible. It had pink ribbons to tie up its sleeves, so the queen saw at once it was a *girl*. When the king knew this he tore his black hair with fury.

"Oh, you silly, silly queen!" he said. "Why didn't I marry a clever lady? Did you think I went to all the trouble and expense of sending you to a witch to get a *girl?* You knew well enough it was a boy I wanted—a boy, an heir, a prince—to learn all my magic and enchantments, and to rule the kingdom after me. I'll bet a crown—my crown," he said, "you never even thought to tell the witch what kind you wanted! Did you now?"

And the queen hung her head and had to confess that she had only asked for a child.

"Very well, madam," said the king, "very well—have your own way. And make the most of your daughter, while she is a child."

The queen did. All the years of her life had never held half so much happiness as now lived in each of the moments when she held her little baby in her arms. And the years went on, and the king grew more and more clever at magic and more and more disagreeable at home, and the princess grew more beautiful and more dear every day she lived.

The queen and the princess were feeding the goldfish in the courtyard fountains with crumbs of the princess's eighteenth birthday cake, when the king came into the courtyard, looking as black as thunder, with his black raven hopping after him. He shook his fist at his family, as indeed he generally did whenever he met them, for he was not a king with pretty home manners. The raven sat down on the edge of the marble basin and tried to peck the goldfish. It was all he could do to show that he was in the same temper as his master.

"A girl indeed!" said the king angrily. "I wonder you can dare to look me in the face, when you remember how your silliness has spoiled everything."

"You shouldn't speak to my mother like that," said the princess. She was eighteen, and it came to her suddenly and all in a moment that she was grown up, so she spoke out.

The king could not utter a word for several

minutes. He was too angry. But the queen said, "My dear child, don't interfere," quite crossly, for she was frightened. And to her husband she said, "My dear, why do you go on worrying about it? Our daughter is not a boy, it is true—but she may marry a clever man who could rule your kingdom after you, and learn as much magic as ever you cared to teach him."

Then the king found his tongue. "If she *does* marry," he said slowly, "her husband will have to be a *very* clever man—oh, yes, very clever indeed! And he will have to know a very great deal more magic than *I* shall ever care to teach him."

The queen knew at once by the king's tone that he was going to be disagreeable. "Ah," she said, "don't punish the child because she loves her mother."

"I'm not going to punish her for *that*," said he. "I'm only going to teach her to respect her father."

And without another word he went off to his laboratory and worked all night, boiling different-colored things in crucibles, and copying charms in curious twisted letters from old brown books with mold stains on their yellowy pages.

The next day his plan was all arranged. He took the poor princess to the Lone Tower, which stands on an island in the sea, a thousand miles from everywhere. He gave her a dowry, and settled a handsome income on her. He engaged a competent dragon to look after her, and also a respectable griffin whose birth and bringing-up he knew all about.

And he said, "Here you shall stay, my dear, respectful daughter, till the clever man comes to marry you. He'll have to be clever enough to sail a ship through the nine whirlpools that spin round the island, and to kill the dragon and the griffin. Till he comes you'll never get any older or any wiser. No doubt he will soon come. You can employ yourself in embroidering your wedding gown. I wish you joy, my dutiful child.''

And his car, drawn by live thunderbolts (thunder travels very fast), rose in the air and disappeared, and the poor princess was left, with the dragon and the griffin, in the Island of the Nine Whirlpools.

The queen, left at home, cried for a day and a night, and then she remembered the witch and called to her. And the witch came, and the queen told her all.

''For the sake of the twice twenty-five kisses you gave me,'' said the witch, ''I will help you. But it is the last thing I can do, and it is not much. Your daughter is under a spell, and I can take you to her. But if I do, you will have to be turned to stone, and to stay so till the spell is taken off the child.''

''I would be a stone for a thousand years,'' said the poor queen, ''if at the end of them I could see my dear again.''

So the witch took the queen in a car drawn by live sunbeams (which travel more quickly than anything else in the world, and much quicker than thunder), and so away and away to the Lone Tower on the Island of the Nine Whirlpools. And there was the princess sitting on the floor in the best room of the Lone Tower, crying as if her heart would break, and the dragon and the griffin were sitting primly on each side of her.

"Oh, mother, mother, mother," she cried, and hung round the queen's neck as if she would never let go.

"Now," said the witch, when they had all cried as much as was good for them, "I can do one or two other little things for you. Time shall not make the princess sad. All days will be like one day till her deliverer comes. And you and I, dear queen, will sit in stone at the gate of the tower. In doing this for you I lose all my witch's powers, and when I say the spell that changes you to stone, I shall change with you, and if ever we come out of the stone, I shall be a witch no more, but only a happy old woman."

Then the three kissed each other again and again; and the witch said the spell, and on each side of the door there was now a stone lady. One of them had a stone crown on its head and a stone scepter in its hand, but the other held a stone tablet with words on it, which the griffin and the dragon could not read, though they had both had a very good education.

And now all days seemed like one day to the princess, and the next day always seemed the day when her mother would come out of the stone and kiss her again. And the years went slowly by.

The wicked king died, and someone else took his kingdom, and many things were changed in the world; but the island did not change, nor the nine whirlpools, nor the griffin, nor the dragon, nor the two stone ladies. And all the time, from the very first, the day of the princess's deliverance was coming, creeping nearer, and nearer, and nearer. But no one saw it coming except the princess, and she only in dreams. And the years went by in tens and in hundreds, and still the nine whirlpools spun round, roaring in triumph the story of many a good ship that had gone down in their swirl, bearing with it some prince who had tried to win the princess and her dowry. And the great sea knew all the other stories of the princes who had come from very far, and had seen the whirlpools, and had shaken their wise young heads and said "'Bout ship!" and gone discreetly home to their nice, safe, comfortable kingdoms.

But no one told the story of the deliverer who was to come. And the years went by.

Now, after more scores of years than you would like to add up on your slate, a certain sailor boy sailed on the high seas with his uncle, who was a skilled skipper. And the boy could reef a sail, and coil a rope, and keep the ship's nose steady before the wind. And he was as good a boy as you would find in a month of Sundays, and worthy to be a prince.

Now, there is Something which is wiser than all the world—and it knows when people are worthy to be princes. And this Something came from the farther side of the seventh world, and whispered in the boy's ear.

And the boy heard, though he did not know he heard, and he looked out over the black sea with the white foam horses galloping over it, and far away he saw a light.

And he said to the skipper, his uncle, "What light is that?"

Then the skipper said, "All good things defend you, Nigel, from sailing near that light. It is not mentioned in all charts, but it is marked in the old chart I steer by, which was my father's father's before me, and his father's father's before him. It is the light that shines from the Lone Tower that stands above the nine whirlpools. And when my father's father was young he heard from the very old man, his great-great-grandfather, that in that tower an enchanted princess, fairer than the day, waits to be delivered. But there is no deliverance, so never steer that way. And think no more of the princess, for that is only an idle tale. But the whirlpools are quite real."

So of course from that day Nigel thought of nothing else. And as he sailed hither and thither upon the high seas, he saw from time to time the light that shone out to sea across the wild swirl of the nine whirlpools. And one night, when the ship was at anchor and the skipper asleep in his bunk Nigel launched the ship's boat and steered alone over the dark sea towards the light. He dared not go very near till daylight should show him what, indeed, were the whirlpools he had to dread.

But when the dawn came he saw the Lone Tower stand dark against the pink and primrose of the east, and about its base the sullen swirl of black water, and he heard the wonderful roar of it. So he hung off and on, and all that day and for six days besides. And when he had watched seven days he knew something. For you are certain to know something if you give for seven days your whole thought to it, even though it be only the first declension or the nine-times table, or the dates of the Norman kings.

What he knew was this: that for five minutes out of the 1,440 minutes that make up a day the whirlpools slipped into silence, while the tide went down and left the yellow sand bare. And every day this happened, but every day it was five minutes earlier than it had been the day before. He made sure of this by the ship's chronometer, which he had thoughtfully brought with him.

So on the eighth day at five minutes before noon Nigel got ready. And when the whirlpools suddenly stopped whirling and the tide sank, like water in a basin that has a hole in it, he stuck to his oars and put his back into his stroke, and presently beached the boat on the yellow sand. Then he dragged her into a cave, and sat down to wait.

By five minutes and one second past noon, the whirlpools were black and busy again, and Nigel peeped out of his cave. And on the rocky ledge overhanging the sea he saw a princess as beautiful as the day, with golden hair and a green gown— and he went out to meet her.

"I've come to save you," he said. "How darling and beautiful you are!"

"You are very good, and very clever, and very dear," said the princess, smiling and giving him both her hands.

He shut a little kiss in each hand before he let them go.

"So now, when the tide is low again, I will take you away in my boat," he said.

"But what about the dragon and the griffin?" asked the princess.

"Dear me," said Nigel. "I didn't know about them. I suppose I can kill them?"

"Don't be a silly boy," said the princess, pretending to be very grown-up, for though she had been on the island time only knows how many years, she was still only eighteen, and she still liked pretending. "You haven't a sword, or a shield, or anything!"

"Well, don't the beasts ever go to sleep?"

"Why, yes," said the princess, "but only once in twenty-four hours, and then the dragon is turned to stone. But the griffin has dreams. The griffin sleeps at teatime every day, but the dragon sleeps every day for five minutes, and every day it is three minutes later than it was the day before."

"What time does he sleep today?" asked Nigel.

"At eleven," said the princess.

"Ah," said Nigel, "can you do sums?"

"No," said the princess, sadly. "I was never good at them."

"Then I must," said Nigel. "I can, but it's slow work, and it makes me very unhappy. It'll take me days and days."

"Don't begin yet," said the princess. "You'll have plenty of time to be unhappy in when I'm not with you. Tell me all about yourself."

So he did. And then she told him all about herself.

"I know I've been here a long time," she said, "but I don't know what time is. And I am very busy sewing silk flowers in a golden gown for my wedding day. And the griffin does the housework —his wings are so convenient and feathery for sweeping and dusting. And the dragon does the cooking: he's hot inside, so of course it's no trouble to him. And though I don't know what time is I'm sure it's time for my wedding-day, because my golden gown only wants one more white daisy on the sleeve, and a lily on the bosom of it, and then it will be ready."

Just then they heard a dry, rustling clatter on the rocks above them and a snorting sound.

"It's the dragon," said the princess, hurriedly.

"Good-bye. Be a good boy, and get your sum done." And she ran away and left him to his arithmetic.

Now the sum was this: "If the whirlpools stop and the tide goes down once in every twenty-four hours, and does it five minutes earlier every twenty-four hours, and if the dragon sleeps every day, and does it three minutes later every day, in how many days and at what time in the day will the tide go down three minutes before the dragon falls asleep?"

It is quite a simple sum, as you see. *You* could do it in a minute because you have been to a good school and have taken pains with your lessons, but it was quite otherwise with poor Nigel. He sat down to work out his sum with a piece of chalk on a smooth stone. He tried it by practice and the unitary method, by multiplication, and by rule-of-three-and-three-quarters. He tried it by decimals and by compound interest. He tried it by square root and by cube root. He tried it by addition, simple and otherwise, and he tried it by mixed examples in vulgar fractions. But it was all of no use. Then he tried to do the sum by algebra, by simple and by quadratic equations, by trigonometry, by logarithms, and by conic sections. But it would not do. He got an answer every time, it is true, but it was always a different one, and he could not feel sure which answer was right.

And just as he was feeling how much more important than anything else it is to be able to do your sums, the princess came back. And now it was getting dark.

"Why, you've been seven hours over that sum," she said, "and you haven't done it yet.

Look here, this is what is written on the tablet of the statue by the lower gate. It has figures in it. Perhaps it is the answer to the sum.''

She held out to him a big white magnolia leaf. And she had scratched on it with the pin of her pearl brooch, and it had turned brown where she had scratched it, as magnolia leaves will do. Nigel read:

> AFTER NINE DAYS
> T 11. 24.
> D 11. 27 Ans.
> P.S.—And the griffin is artificial. R.

He clapped his hands softly.

''Dear Princess,'' he said, ''I know that's the right answer. It says R, too, you see. But I'll just prove it.'' So he hastily worked the sum backwards in equations and conic sections, and all the rules he could think of. And it came right every time.

''So now we must wait,'' said he. And they waited.

And every day the princess came to see Nigel and brought him food cooked by the dragon, and he lived in his cave, and talked to her when she was there, and thought about her when she was not, and they were both as happy as the longest day in summer. Then at last came The Day. Nigel and the princess laid their plans.

''You're sure he won't hurt *you*, my only treasure?'' said Nigel.

''Quite,'' said the princess. ''I only wish I were half as sure that he wouldn't hurt *you*.''

"My princess," he said tenderly, "two great powers are on our side: the power of love and the power of arithmetic. Those two are stronger than anything else in the world."

So when the tide began to go down Nigel and the princess ran out onto the sands, and there, full in sight of the terrace where the dragon kept watch, Nigel took his princess in his arms and kissed her. The griffin was busy sweeping the stairs of the Lone Tower, but the dragon saw, and gave a cry of rage—and it was like twenty engines all letting off steam at the top of their voices inside Cannon Street Station.

And the two lovers stood looking up at the dragon. He was dreadful to look at. His head was white with age—and his beard had grown so long that he caught his claws in it as he walked. His wings were white with the salt that had settled on them from the spray of the sea. His tail was long and thick and joined and white, and had little legs to it, any number of them—far too many—so that it looked like a very large fat silkworm. And his claws were as long as lessons and as sharp as bayonets.

"Good-bye, love!" cried Nigel and ran out across the yellow sand toward the sea. He had one end of a cord tied to his arm.

The dragon was clambering down the face of the cliff, and next moment he was crawling and writhing and sprawling and wriggling across the beach after Nigel, making great holes in the sand with his heavy feet—and the very end of his tail, where there were no legs, made, as it dragged, a mark in the sand such as you make when you launch a boat. And he breathed fire till the wet sand hissed again, and the water of the little rock pools got quite frightened, and all went off in steam.

And still Nigel held on and the dragon after him.

The princess could see nothing for the steam, and she stood crying bitterly, but still holding on tight with her right hand to the other end of the cord which Nigel had told her to hold, while with her left she held the ship's chronometer, and looked at it through her tears as he had bidden her look, so as to know when to pull the rope.

On went Nigel over the sand, and on went the dragon after him. And the tide was low, and sleepy little waves lapped the sand's edge.

Now at the lip of the water Nigel paused and looked back, and the dragon made a bound, beginning a scream of rage that was like all the engines of all the railways in England. But it never uttered the second half of that scream, for now it knew suddenly that it was sleepy—it turned to hurry back to dry land, because sleeping near whirlpools is so unsafe. But before it reached the shore sleep caught it and turned it to stone. And Nigel, seeing this, ran shoreward for his life—and the tide began to flow in, and the time of the whirlpools' sleep was nearly over, and he stumbled and he waded and he swam, and the princess pulled for dear life at the cord in her hand, and pulled him up onto the dry shelf of rock just as the great sea dashed in and made itself once more into the girdle of nine whirlpools all round the island.

But the dragon was asleep under the whirlpools, and when he woke up from being asleep he found he was drowned, so there was an end of him.

"Now there's only the griffin," said Nigel.

And the princess said, "Yes—only—" And she kissed Nigel and went back to sew the last leaf of the the lily on the bosom of her wedding gown. And she thought and thought of what was written on the stone about the griffin being artificial—and the next day she said to Nigel, "You know a griffin is half a lion and half an eagle, and the other two halves when they've joined make the leo-griff. But I've never seen *him*. Yet I have an idea."

So they talked it over and arranged everything.

Then when the griffin fell asleep that afternoon at teatime, Nigel went softly behind him and trod on his tail, and at the same time the princess cried, "Look out! There's a lion behind you."

And the griffin, waking suddenly from his dreams, twisted his large neck round to look for the lion, and saw a lion's flank, and fastened its eagle beak in it. For the griffin had been artificially made by the king-enchanter, and the two halves had never really got used to each other. So now the eagle half of the griffin, who was still rather sleepy, believed that it was fighting a lion, and the lion part, being half asleep, thought it was fighting an eagle, and the whole griffin in its deep drowsiness hadn't the sense to pull itself together and remember what it was made of. So the griffin rolled over and over, one end of it fighting with the other, till the eagle end pecked the lion end to death, and the lion end tore the eagle end with its claws till it died. And so the griffin that was made of a lion and an eagle perished, exactly as if it had been made of Kilkenny cats.

"Poor griffin," said the princess, "it was very good at the housework. I always liked it better than the dragon: it wasn't so hot-tempered."

And at that moment there was a soft, silky rush behind the princess, and there was her mother, the queen, who had slipped out of the stone statue directly after the griffin was dead, and now came hurrying to take her dear daughter in her arms. The witch was clambering slowly off her pedestal. She was a little stiff with standing still so long.

When they had all explained everything over and over to each other as many times as was good for them, the witch said, "Well, but what about the whirlpools?"

And Nigel said he didn't know.

Then the witch said, "I'm not a witch anymore. I'm only a happy old woman, but I know some things still. Those whirlpools were made by the enchanter-king's dropping nine drops of his blood into the sea. And his blood was so wicked that the sea has been trying ever since to get rid of it, and that made the whirlpools. Now you've only got to go out at low tide—"

So Nigel understood and went out at low tide, and found in the sandy hollow left by the first whirlpool a great red ruby. And that was the first drop of the wicked king's blood. And next day Nigel found another, and next day another, and so on till the ninth day, and then the sea was as smooth as glass.

The nine rubies were used afterwards in agriculture. You had only to throw them out into a field if you wanted it plowed. Then the whole surface land turned itself over in its anxiety to get rid of something so wicked, and in the morning the field was found to be plowed as thoroughly as any young man at Oxford. So the wicked king did some good after all.

When the sea was smooth, ships came from far and wide bringing people to hear the wonderful story. And a beautiful palace was built, and the princess was married to Nigel in her gold dress, and they all lived happily as long as was good for them.

The dragon still lies, a stone dragon on the sand, and at low tide the little children play round him and over him. But the pieces that were left of the griffin were buried under the herb bed in the palace garden, because it had been so good at housework, and it wasn't its fault that it had been made so badly and put to such poor work as guarding a lady from her lover.

I have no doubt that you will wish to know what the princess lived on during the long years when the dragon did the cooking. My dear, she lived on her income, and that is a thing which a great many people would like to be able to do.

Chapter 6

The Dragon Tamers

There was once an old, old castle. It was so old that its walls and towers and turrets and gateways and arches had crumbled to ruins, and of all its old splendor there were only two little rooms left, and it was here that John the blacksmith had set up his forge.

He was too poor to live in a proper house, and no one asked any rent for the rooms in the ruin, because all the lords of the castle were dead and gone this many a year. So there John blew his bellows, and hammered his iron, and did all the work which came his way.

This was not much, because most of the trade went to the mayor of the town, who was also a blacksmith in quite a large way of business, and had his huge forge facing the square of the town, and had twelve apprentices, all hammering like a nest of woodpeckers, and twelve journeymen to order the apprentices about, and a patent forge and a self-acting hammer and electric bellows, and all things handsome about him. So that of course the townspeople, whenever they wanted a horse shod or a shaft mended, went to the mayor. And John the blacksmith struggled on as best he could, with a few odd jobs from travelers and strangers who did not know what a superior forge the mayor's was.

The two rooms were warm and weathertight, but not very large, so the blacksmith got into the way of keeping his old iron, and his odds and ends, and his fagots, and his twopenn'orths of coal, in the great dungeon down under the castle. It was a very fine dungeon indeed, with a handsome vaulted roof and big iron rings, whose staples were built into the wall, very strong and convenient for tying captives up to, and at one end was a broken flight of wide steps leading down no one knew where.

Even the lords of the castle in the good old times had never known where those steps led to, but every now and then they would kick a prisoner down the steps in their lighthearted, hopeful way, and sure enough, the prisoners never came back. The blacksmith had never dared to go beyond the seventh step, and no more have I —so I know no more than he did what was at the bottom of those stairs.

John the blacksmith had a wife and a little baby. When his wife was not doing the housework she used to nurse the baby and cry, remembering the happy days when she lived with her father, who kept seventeen cows and lived quite in the country, and when John used to come courting her in the summer evenings, as smart as smart, with a posy in his buttonhole. And now John's hair was getting gray, and there was hardly ever enough to eat.

As for the baby, it cried a good deal at odd times, but at night, when its mother had settled down to sleep, it would always begin to cry, quite as a matter of course, so that she hardly got any rest at all. This made her very tired. The baby could make up for its bad nights during the day, if it liked, but the poor mother couldn't. So whenever she had nothing to do she used to sit and cry, because she was tired out with work and worry.

One evening the blacksmith was busy with his forge. He was making a goatshoe for the goat of a very rich lady, who wished to see how the goat liked being shod, and also whether the shoe would come to fivepence or sevenpence before she ordered the whole set. This was the only order John had had that week. And as he worked, his wife sat and nursed the baby, who, for a wonder, was not crying.

Presently, over the noise of the bellows, and over the clank of the iron, there came another sound. The blacksmith and his wife looked at each other.

"I heard nothing," said he.

"Neither did I," said she.

But the noise grew louder—and the two were so anxious not to hear it that he hammered away at the goatshoe harder than he had ever hammered in his life, and she began to sing to the baby—a thing she had not had the heart to do for weeks.

But through the blowing and hammering and singing the noise came louder and louder, and the more they tried not to hear it, the more they had to. It was like the noise of some great creature purring, purring, purring—and the reason they did not want to believe they really heard it was that it came from the great dungeon down below, where the old iron was, and the firewood and the twopenn'orth of coal, and the broken steps that went down into the dark and ended no one knew where.

"It *can't* be anything in the dungeon," said the blacksmith, wiping his face. "Why, I shall have to go down there after more coals in a minute."

"There isn't anything there, of course. How could there be?" said his wife. And they tried so hard to believe that there could be nothing there that presently they very nearly did believe it.

Then the blacksmith took his shovel in one hand and his riveting hammer in the other, and hung the old stable lantern on his little finger, and went down to get the coals.

"I am not taking the hammer because I think there is anything there," said he, "but it is handy for breaking the large lumps of coal."

"I quite understand," said his wife, who had brought the coal home in her apron that afternoon, and knew that it was all coal dust.

So he went down the winding stairs to the dungeon, and stood at the bottom of the steps holding the lantern above his head just to see that the dungeon really *was* empty, as usual. Half of it was empty as usual, except for the old iron and odds and ends, and the firewood and the coals. But the other side was not empty. It was quite full, and what it was full of was *Dragon*.

"It must have come up those nasty broken steps from goodness knows where," said the blacksmith to himself, trembling all over, as he tried to creep back up the winding stairs.

But the dragon was too quick for him—it put out a great claw and caught him by the leg, and as it moved it rattled like a great bunch of keys, or like the sheet iron they make thunder out of in pantomimes.

"No you don't," said the dragon, in a sputtering voice, like a damp squib.

"Deary, deary me," said poor John, trembling more than ever in the claw of the dragon. "Here's a nice end for a respectable blacksmith!"

The dragon seemed very much struck by this remark.

"Do you mind saying that again?" said he, quite politely.

So John said again, very distinctly, "Here—Is—A—Nice—End—For—A—Respectable—Blacksmith."

"I didn't know," said the dragon. "Fancy now! You're the very man I wanted."

"So I understood you to say before," said John, his teeth chattering.

"Oh, I don't mean what you mean," said the dragon, "but I should like you to do a job for me. One of my wings has got some of the rivets out of it just above the joint. Could you put that to rights?"

"I might, sir," said John, politely, for you must always be polite to a possible customer, even if he be a dragon.

"A master craftsman—you *are* a master, of course?—can see in a minute what's wrong," the dragon went on. "Just come round here and feel of my plates, will you?"

John timidly went round when the dragon took his claw away, and sure enough, the dragon's off wing was hanging loose and all anyhow, and several of the plates near the joint certainly wanted riveting.

The dragon seemed to be made almost entirely of iron armor—a sort of tawny, red-rust color it was; from damp, no doubt—and under it he seemed to be covered with something furry.

All the blacksmith welled up in John's heart, and he felt more at ease. "You could certainly do with a rivet or two, sir," said he. "In fact, you want a good many."

"Well, get to work, then," said the dragon. "You mend my wing, and then I'll go out and eat up all the town, and if you make a really smart job of it I'll eat you last. There!"

"I don't want to be eaten last, sir," said John.

"Well, then, I'll eat you *first*," said the dragon.

"I don't want that, sir, either," said John.

"Go on with you, you silly man," said the dragon. "You don't know your own silly mind. Come, set to work."

"I don't like the job, sir," said John, "and that's the truth. I know how easily accidents happen. It's all fair and smooth, and 'Please rivet me, and I'll eat you last'—and then you get to work and you give a gentleman a bit of a nip or a dig under his rivets—and then it's fire and smoke, and no apologies will meet the case."

"Upon my word of honor as a dragon," said the other.

"I know you wouldn't do it on purpose, sir," said John, "but any gentleman will give a jump and a sniff if he's nipped, and one of your sniffs would be enough for me. Now, if you'd just let me fasten you up?"

"It would be so undignified," objected the dragon.

"We always fasten a horse up," said John, "and he's the 'noble animal.' "

"It's all very well," said the dragon, "but how do I know you'd untie me again when you'd riveted me? Give me something in pledge. What do you value most?"

"My hammer," said John. "A blacksmith is nothing without a hammer."

"But you'd want that for riveting me. You must think of something else, and at once, or I'll eat you first."

At this moment the baby in the room above began to scream. Its mother had been so quiet that it thought she had settled down for the night, and that it was time to begin.

"Whatever's that?" said the dragon—starting so that every plate on his body rattled.

"It's only the baby," said John.

"What's that?' asked the dragon. "Something you value?"

"Well, yes, sir, rather," said the blacksmith.

"Then bring it here," said the dragon, "and I'll take care of it till you've done riveting me, and you shall tie me up."

"All right, sir," said John, "but I ought to warn you. Babies are poison to dragons, so I don't deceive you. It's all right to touch—but don't you go putting it into your mouth. I shouldn't like to see any harm come to a nice-looking gentleman like you.''

The dragon purred at this compliment and said, ''All right, I'll be careful. Now go and fetch the thing, whatever it is.''

So John ran up the steps as quickly as he could, for he knew that if the dragon got impatient before it was fastened up, it could heave up the roof of the dungeon with one heave of its back, and kill them all in the ruins. His wife was asleep, in spite of the baby's cries, and John picked up the baby and took it down and put it between the dragon's front paws.

''You just purr to it, sir,'' he said, ''and it'll be as good as gold.''

So the dragon purred, and his purring pleased the baby so much that it left off crying.

Then John rummaged among the heap of old iron and found there some heavy chains and a great collar that had been made in the days when men sang over their work and put their hearts into it, so that the things they made were strong enough to bear the weight of a thousand years, let alone a dragon.

John fastened the dragon up with the collar and the chains, and when he had padlocked them all on safely, he set to work to find out how many rivets would be needed.

''Six, eight, ten—twenty, forty,'' said he. ''I haven't half enough rivets in the shop. If you'll excuse me, sir, I'll step round to another forge and get a few dozen. I won't be a minute.''

And off he went, leaving the baby between the dragon's forepaws, laughing and crowing with pleasure at the very large purr of it.

John ran as hard as he could into the town, and found the mayor and corporation.

"There's a dragon in my dungeon," he said. "I've chained him up. Now come and help to get my baby away."

And he told them all about it.

But they all happened to have engagements for that evening, so they praised John's cleverness, and said they were quite content to leave the matter in his hands.

"But what about my baby?" said John.

"Oh, well," said the mayor, "if anything should happen, you will always be able to remember that your baby perished in a good cause."

So John went home again and told his wife some of the tale.

"You've given the baby to the dragon!" she cried. "Oh, you unnatural parent!"

"Hush," said John, and he told her some more.

"Now," he said, "I'm going down. After I've been down you can go, and if you keep your head the boy will be all right."

So down went the blacksmith, and there was the dragon purring away with all his might to keep the baby quiet.

"Hurry up, can't you?" he said. "I can't keep up this noise all night."

"I'm very sorry, sir," said the blacksmith, "but all the shops are shut. The job must wait till the morning. And don't forget you've promised to take care of that baby. You'll find it a little wearing, I'm afraid. Good night, sir."

The dragon had purred till he was quite out of

breath—so now he stopped, and as soon as everything was quiet the baby thought everyone must have settled for the night, and that it was time to begin to scream. So it began.

"Oh, dear," said the dragon, "this is awful."

He patted the baby with his claw, but it screamed more than ever.

"And I am so tired, too," said the dragon. "I did so hope I should have had a good night."

The baby went on screaming.

"There'll be no peace for me after this," said the dragon. "It's enough to ruin one's nerves. Hush, then—did 'ums, then." And he tried to quiet the baby as if it had been a young dragon. But when he began to sing "Hush-a-by, dragon," the baby screamed more and more and more. "I can't keep it quiet," said the dragon. And then suddenly he saw a woman sitting on the steps. "Here, I say," said he, "do you know anything about babies?"

"I do, a little," said the mother.

"Then I wish you'd take this one, and let me get some sleep," said the dragon, yawning. "You can bring it back in the morning before the blacksmith comes."

So the mother picked up the baby and took it upstairs and told her husband, and they went to bed happy, for they had caught the dragon and saved the baby.

And next day John went down and explained carefully to the dragon exactly how matters stood, and he got an iron gate with a grating to it, and set it up at the foot of the steps, and the dragon mewed furiously for days and days, but when he found it was no good he was quiet.

So now John went to the mayor, and said, "I've got the dragon and I've saved the town."

"Noble preserver," cried the mayor, "we will get up a subscription for you, and crown you in public with a laurel wreath."

So the mayor put his name down for five pounds, and the corporation each gave three, and other people gave their guineas and half guineas, and half crowns and crowns, and while the subscription was being made the mayor ordered three poems at his own expense from the town poet to celebrate the occasion. The poems were very much admired, especially by the mayor and corporation.

The first poem dealt with the noble conduct of the mayor in arranging to have the dragon tied up. The second described the splendid assistance rendered by the corporation. And the third expressed the pride and joy of the poet in being permitted to sing such deeds, beside which the actions of St. George must appear quite commonplace to all with feeling heart or a well-balanced brain.

When the subscription was finished there was a thousand pounds, and a committee was formed to settle what should be done with it. A third of it went to pay for a banquet to the mayor and corporation; another third was spent in buying a gold collar with a dragon on it for the mayor, and gold medals with dragons on them for the corporation; and what was left went in committee expenses.

So there was nothing for the blacksmith except the laurel wreath, and the knowledge that it really *was* he who had saved the town. But after this things went a little better with the blacksmith. To begin with, the baby did not cry so much as it had before. Then the rich lady who owned the goat was so touched by John's noble action that she ordered a complete set of shoes at two shillings, fourpence, and even made it up to two shillings, sixpence, in grateful recognition of his public-spirited conduct. Then tourists used to come in breaks from quite a long way off, and pay twopence each to go down the steps and peep through the iron grating at the rusty dragon in the dungeon—and it was threepence extra for each party if the blacksmith let off colored fire to see it by, which, as the fire was extremely short, was twopence-halfpenny clear profit every time. And the blacksmith's wife used to provide teas at ninepence a head, and altogether things grew brighter week by week.

The baby—named John, after his father, and called Johnnie for short—began presently to grow up. He was great friends with Tina, the daughter of the whitesmith, who lived nearly opposite. She was a dear little girl, with yellow pigtails and blue eyes, and she was never tired of hearing the story of how Johnnie, when he was a baby, had been minded by a real dragon.

The two children used to go together to peep through the iron grating at the dragon, and sometimes they would hear him mew piteously. And they would light a halfpennyworth of colored fire to look at him by. And they grew older and wiser.

Now, at last one day the mayor and corporation, hunting the hare in their gold gowns, came screaming back to the town gates with news that a lame, humpy giant, as big as a tin church, was coming over the marshes towards the town.

"We're lost," said the mayor. "I'd give a thousand pounds to anyone who could keep that giant out of the town. *I* know what he eats—by his teeth."

No one seemed to know what to do. But Johnnie and Tina were listening, and they looked at each other, and then ran off as fast as their boots would carry them.

They ran through the forge, and down the dungeon steps, and knocked at the iron door.

"Who's there?" said the dragon.

"It's only us," said the children.

And the dragon was so dull from having been alone for ten years that he said, "Come in, dears."

"You won't hurt us, or breathe fire at us or anything?" asked Tina.

And the dragon said, "Not for worlds."

So they went in and talked to him, and told him what the weather was like outside, and what there was in the papers, and at last Johnnie said, "There's a lame giant in the town. He wants you."

"Does he?" said the dragon, showing his teeth. "If only I were out of this!"

"If we let you loose you might manage to run away before he could catch you."

"Yes, I *might*," answered the dragon, "but then again I mightn't."

"Why—you'd never fight him?" said Tina.

"No," said the dragon. "I'm all for peace, I am. You let me out, and you'll see."

So the children loosed the dragon from the

chains and the collar, and he broke down one end of the dungeon and went out—only pausing at the forge door to get the blacksmith to rivet his wing.

He met the lame giant at the gate of the town, and the giant banged on the dragon with his club as if he were banging an iron foundry, and the dragon behaved like a smelting works—all fire and smoke. It was a fearful sight, and people watched it from a distance, falling off their legs with the shock of every bang, but always getting up to look again.

At last the dragon won, and the giant sneaked away across the marshes, and the dragon, who was very tired, went home to sleep, announcing his intention of eating the town in the morning. He went back into his old dungeon because he was a stranger in the town, and he did not know of any other respectable lodging. Then Tina and Johnnie went to the mayor and corporation and said, "The giant is settled. Please give us the thousand pounds reward."

But the mayor said, "No, no, my boy. It is not you who have settled the giant, it is the dragon. I suppose you have chained him up again? When *he* comes to claim the reward he shall have it."

"He isn't chained up yet," said Johnnie. "Shall I send him to claim the reward?"

But the mayor said he need not trouble, and now he offered a thousand pounds to anyone who would get the dragon chained up again.

"I don't trust you," said Johnnie. "Look how you treated my father when he chained up the dragon."

But the people who were listening at the door

interrupted, and said that if Johnnie could fasten up the dragon again they would turn out the mayor and let Johnnie be mayor in his place. For they had been dissatisfied with the mayor for some time, and thought they would like a change.

So Johnnie said, "Done," and off he went, hand in hand with Tina, and they called on all their little friends and said, "Will you help us save the town?"

And all the children said, "Yes, of course we will. What fun!"

"Well, then," said Tina, "you must all bring your basins of bread and milk to the forge tomorrow at breakfast time."

"And if ever I am mayor," said Johnnie, "I will give a banquet, and you shall all be invited. And we'll have nothing but sweet things from beginning to end."

All the children promised, and next morning Tina and Johnnie rolled the big washing tub down the winding stair.

"What's that noise?" asked the dragon.

"It's only a big giant breathing," said Tina. "He's gone by, now."

Then, when all the town children brought their bread and milk, Tina emptied it into the washtub, and when the tub was full Tina knocked at the iron door with the grating in it, and said, "May we come in?"

"Oh, yes," said the dragon; "it's very dull here."

So they went in, and with the help of nine other children they lifted the washing tub in and set it down by the dragon. Then all the other children went away, and Tina and Johnnie sat down and cried.

"What's this?" asked the dragon. "And what's the matter?"

"*This* is bread and milk," said Johnnie. "It's our breakfast—all of it."

"Well," said the dragon, "I don't see what you want with breakfast. I'm going to eat everyone in the town as soon as I've rested a little."

"Dear Mr. Dragon," said Tina, "I wish you wouldn't eat us. How would you like to be eaten yourself?"

"Not at all," the dragon confessed, "but nobody will eat me."

"I don't know," said Johnnie, "there's a giant—"

"I know. I fought with him, and licked him—"

"Yes, but there's another come now—the one you fought was only this one's little boy. This one is half as big again."

"He's seven times as big," said Tina.

"No, nine times," said Johnnie. "He's bigger than the steeple."

"Oh dear," said the dragon. "I never expected this."

"And the mayor has told him where you are," Tina went on, "and he is coming to eat you as soon as he has sharpened his big knife. The mayor told him you were a wild dragon—but he didn't mind. He said he only ate wild dragons—with bread sauce."

"That's tiresome," said the dragon, "and I suppose this sloppy stuff in the tub is the bread sauce?"

The children said it was. "Of course," they added, "bread sauce is only served with wild dragons. Tame ones are served with apple sauce

113

and onion stuffing. What a pity you're not a tame one: he'd never look at you then," they said. "Good-bye, poor dragon, we shall never see you again, and now you'll know what it's like to be eaten." And they began to cry again.

"Well, but look here," said the dragon, "couldn't you pretend I was a tame dragon? Tell the giant that I'm just a poor little, timid tame dragon that you keep for a pet."

"He'd never believe it," said Johnnie. "If you were our tame dragon we should keep you tied up, you know. We shouldn't like to risk losing such a dear, pretty pet."

Then the dragon begged them to fasten him up at once, and they did so: with a collar and chains that were made years ago—in the days when men sang over their work and made it strong enough to bear any strain.

And then they went away and told the people what they had done, and Johnnie was made mayor, and had a glorious feast exactly as he had said he would—with nothing in it but sweet things. It began with Turkish delight and half-penny buns, and went on with oranges, toffee, coconut ice, peppermints, jam puffs, raspberry noyau, ice creams, and meringues, and ended with bull's-eyes and gingerbread and acid drops.

This was all very well for Johnnie and Tina, but if you are kind children with feeling hearts you will perhaps feel sorry for the poor deceived, deluded dragon—chained up in the dull dungeon, with nothing to do but to think over the shocking untruths that Johnnie had told him.

When he thought how he had been tricked, the poor captive dragon began to weep—and the large tears fell down over his rusty plates. And presently he began to feel faint, as people sometimes do when they have been crying, especially if they have not had anything to eat for ten years or so.

And then the poor creature dried his eyes and looked about him, and there he saw the tub of bread and milk. So he thought, "If giants like this damp, white stuff, perhaps *I* should like it too," and he tasted a little, and liked it so much that he ate it all up.

And the next time the tourists came, and Johnnie let off the colored fire, the dragon said, shyly, "Excuse my troubling you, but could you bring me a little more bread and milk?"

So Johnnie arranged that people should go round with carts every day to collect the children's bread and milk for the dragon. The children were fed at the town's expense—on whatever they liked. And they ate nothing but cakes and buns and sweet things, and they said the poor dragon was very welcome to their bread and milk.

Now, when Johnnie had been mayor ten years or so he married Tina, and on their wedding morning they went to see the dragon. He had grown quite tame, and his rusty plates had fallen off in places, and underneath he was soft and furry to stroke. So now they stroked him.

And he said, "I don't know how I could ever have liked eating anything but bread and milk. I *am* a tame dragon, now, aren't I?" And when they said yes, he was, the dragon said, "I am so tame, won't you undo me?"

And some people would have been afraid to

trust him, but Johnnie and Tina were so happy on their wedding day that they could not believe any harm of anyone in the world. So they loosed the chains, and the dragon said, "Excuse me a moment, there are one or two little things I should like to fetch," and he moved off to those mysterious steps and went down them, out of sight into the darkness. And as he moved, more and more of his rusty plates fell off.

In a few minutes they heard him clanking up the steps. He brought something in his mouth— it was a bag of gold.

"It's no good to me," he said. "Perhaps you might find it come in useful." So they thanked him very kindly.

"More where that came from," said he, and fetched more and more and more, till they told him to stop. So now they were rich, and so were their fathers and mothers. Indeed, everyone was rich, and there were no more poor people in the town. And they all got rich without working, which is very wrong, but the dragon had never been to school, as you have, so he knew no better.

And as the dragon came out of the dungeon, following Johnnie and Tina into the bright gold and blue of their wedding day, he blinked his eyes as a cat does in the sunshine, and he shook himself, and the last of his plates dropped off, and his wings with them, and he was just like a very, very extra-sized cat. And from that day he grew furrier and furrier, and he was the beginning of all cats. Nothing of the dragon remained except the claws, which all cats have still, as you can easily ascertain.

And I hope you see now how important it is to feed your cat with bread and milk. If you were to let it have nothing to eat but mice and birds it might grow larger and fiercer, and scalier and tailier, and get wings and turn into the beginning of dragons. And then there would be all the bother over again.

Chapter 7

The Fiery Dragon, or the Heart of Stone and the Heart of Gold

The little white princess always woke in her little white bed when the starlings began to chatter in the pearl gray morning. As soon as the woods were awake, she used to run up the twisting turret stairs with her little bare feet, and stand on top of the tower in her white bedgown, and kiss her hands to the sun and to the woods and to the sleeping town, and say "Good morning, pretty world!"

Then she would run down the cold stone steps and dress herself in her short skirt and her cap and apron, and begin the day's work. She swept the rooms and made the breakfast, she washed the dishes and she scoured the pans, and all this she did because she was a real princess. For of all who should have served her, only one remained faithful—her old nurse, who had lived with her in the tower all the princess's life. And now the nurse was old and feeble, the princess would not let her work anymore but did all the housework herself, while the Nurse sat still and did the sewing, because this was a real princess with a skin like milk, and hair like flax, and a heart like gold.

Her name was Sabrinetta, and her grandmother was Sabra, who married St. George after he had killed the dragon, and by real rights all the country belonged to her: the woods that stretched away to the mountains, and the downs that sloped down to the sea, and the pretty fields of corn and maize and rye, the olive orchards and the vineyards, and the little town itself with its towers and its turrets, its steep roofs and strange windows, that nestled in the hollow between the sea where the whirlpool was and the mountains, white with snow and rosy with sunrise.

But when her father and mother died, leaving her cousin to take care of the kingdom till she grew up, he, being a very evil prince, had taken everything away from her, and all the people followed him, and now nothing was left her of all her possessions except the great dragonproof tower that her grandfather, St. George, had built, and of all who should have been her servants only the good nurse.

And this was why Sabrinetta was the first person in all the land to get a glimpse of the wonder.

Early, early, early, while all the townspeople were fast asleep, she ran up the turret steps and looked out over the field, and at the other side of the field there is a green-ferny ditch and a rose-thorny hedge, and then comes the wood. And as Sabrinetta stood on her tower she saw a shaking and a twisting of the rose-thorny hedge, and then something very bright and shining wriggled out through it into the ferny ditch and back again.

It only came out for a minute, but she saw it quite plainly, and she said to herself, "Dear me, what a curious, shiny, bright-looking creature! If it were bigger, and if I didn't know that there have been no fabulous monsters for quite a long time now, I should almost think it was a dragon."

The thing, whatever it was, did look rather like a dragon—but then it was too small. And it looked rather like a lizard—only then it was too big. It was about as long as a hearthrug.

"I wish it had not been in such a hurry to get back into the wood," said Sabrinetta. "Of course, it's quite safe for me, in my dragonproof tower, but if it *is* a dragon, it's quite big enough to eat people, and today's the first of May, and the children go out to get flowers in the wood."

When Sabrinetta had done the housework (she did not leave so much as a speck of dust anywhere, even in the corneriest corner of the winding stair) she put on her milk white silky gown with the moon daisies worked on it, and went up to the top of her tower again.

Across the fields troops of children were going out to gather the may, and the sound of their laughter and singing came up to the top of the tower.

"I do hope it *wasn't* a dragon," said Sabrinetta.

The children went by twos and by threes and by tens and twenties, and the red and blue and yellow and white of their frocks were scattered on the green of the field.

"It's like a green silk mantle worked with flowers," said the princess, smiling.

By twos and by threes, by tens and by twenties, the children vanished into the wood, till the mantle of the field was left plain green once more.

120

"All the embroidery is unpicked," said the princess, sighing.

The sun shone, and the sky was blue, and the fields were quite green, and all the flowers were very bright indeed, because it was May Day.

Then quite suddenly a cloud passed over the sun, and the silence was broken by shrieks from afar off. And like a many-colored torrent, all the children burst from the wood, and rushed, a red and blue and yellow and white wave, across the field, screaming as they ran.

Their voices came up to the princess in her tower, and she heard the words threaded on their screams, like beads on sharp needles: "The dragon, the dragon, the dragon! Open the gates! The dragon is coming! The fiery dragon!"

And they swept across the field and into the gate of the town, and the princess heard the gate bang, and the children were out of sight—but on the other side of the field the rose thorns crackled and smashed in the hedge, and something very large and glaring and horrible trampled the ferns in the ditch for one moment before it hid itself again in the covert of the wood.

The princess went down and told her nurse, and the nurse at once locked the great door of the tower and put the key in her pocket.

"Let them take care of themselves," she said, when the princess begged to be allowed to go out and help to take care of the children. "My business is to take care of you, my precious, and I'm going to do it. Old as I am, I can turn a key still."

So Sabrinetta went up again to the top of her tower, and cried whenever she thought of the children and the fiery dragon. For she knew, of course, that the gates of the town were not dragonproof, and that the dragon could just walk in whenever he liked.

The children ran straight to the palace, where the prince was cracking his hunting whip down at the kennels, and told him what had happened.

"Good sport," said the prince, and he ordered out his pack of hippopotamuses at once. It was his custom to hunt big game with hippopotamuses, and people would not have minded that so much—but he would swagger about in the streets of the town with his pack yelping and gamboling at his heels, and when he did that, the greengrocer, who had his stall in the marketplace, always regretted it. And the crockery merchant, who spread his wares on the pavement, was ruined for life every time the prince chose to show off his pack.

The prince rode out of the town with his hippopotamuses trotting and frisking behind him, and people got inside their houses as quickly as they could when they heard the voices of his pack and the blowing of his horn. The pack squeezed through the town gates and off across country to hunt the dragon.

Few of you who have not seen a pack of hippopotamuses in full cry will be able to imagine at all what the hunt was like. To begin with, hippopotamuses do not bay like hounds: they grunt like pigs, and their grunt is very big and fierce. Then, of course, no one expects hippopotamuses to jump. They just crash through the hedges and lumber through the standing corn, doing serious injury to the crops, and annoying the farmers very much.

All the hippopotamuses had collars with their name and address on, but when the farmers called at the palace to complain of the injury to their standing crops, the prince always said it served them right for leaving their crops standing about in people's way, and he never paid anything at all.

So now, when he and his pack went out, several people in the town whispered, "I wish the dragon would eat *him*"—which was very wrong of them, no doubt, but then he was such a very nasty prince.

They hunted by field, and they hunted by wold. They drew the woods blank, and the scent didn't lie on the downs at all. The dragon was shy, and would not show himself.

But just as the prince was beginning to think there was no dragon at all, but only a cock and bull, his favorite old hippopotamus gave tongue.

The prince blew his horn and shouted, "Tally ho! Hark forward! Tantivy!" and the whole pack charged downhill towards the hollow by the wood. For there, plain to be seen, was the dragon, as big as a barge, glowing like a furnace, and spitting fire and showing his shining teeth.

"The hunt is up!" cried the prince. And indeed it was. For the dragon—instead of behaving as a quarry should, and running away—ran straight at the pack, and the prince on his elephant had the mortification of seeing his prize pack swallowed up one by one in the twinkling of an eye, by the dragon they had come out to hunt. The dragon swallowed all the hippopotamuses just as a dog swallows bits of meat.

123

It was a shocking sight. Of the whole of the pack that had come out sporting so merrily to the music of the horn, now not even a puppy hippopotamus was left, and the dragon was looking anxiously round to see if he had forgotten anything.

The prince slipped off his elephant on the other side, and ran into the thickest part of the wood. He hoped the dragon could not break through the bushes there, since they were very strong and close. He went crawling on hands and knees in a most unprincelike way, and at last, finding a hollow tree, he crept into it.

The wood was very still—no crashing of branches and no smell of burning came to alarm the prince. He drained the silver hunting bottle slung from his shoulder, and stretched his legs in the hollow tree. He never shed a single tear for his poor tame hippopotamuses who had eaten from his hand and followed him faithfully in all the pleasures of the chase for so many years. For he was a false prince, with a skin like leather and hair like hearth brushes, and a heart like a stone.

He never shed a tear, but he just went to sleep. When he awoke it was dark. He crept out of the tree and rubbed his eyes. The wood was black about him, but there was a red glow in a dell close by, and it was a fire of sticks, and beside it sat a ragged youth with long, yellow hair; all round lay sleeping forms which breathed heavily.

"Who are you?" said the prince.

"I'm Elfinn, the pigkeeper," said the ragged youth. "And who are you?"

"I'm Tiresome, the prince," said the other.

"And what are you doing out of your palace at this time of night?" asked the pigkeeper severely.

"I've been hunting," said the prince.

The pigkeeper laughed. "Oh, it was you I saw, then? A good hunt, wasn't it? My pigs and I were looking on."

All the sleeping forms grunted and snored, and the prince saw that they were pigs: he knew it by their manners.

"If you had known as much as I do," Elfinn went on, "you might have saved your pack."

"What do you mean?" said Tiresome.

"Why, the dragon," said Elfinn. "You went out at the wrong time of day. The dragon should be hunted at *night*."

"No, thank you," said the prince with a shudder. "A daylight hunt is quite good enough for me, you silly pigkeeper."

"Oh, well," said Elfinn, "do as you like about it—the dragon will come and hunt *you* tomorrow, as likely as not. I don't care if he does, you silly prince."

"You're very rude," said Tiresome.

"Oh, no, only truthful," said Elfinn.

"Well, tell me the truth, then. What is it that if I had known as much as you do about I shouldn't have lost my hippopotamuses?"

"You don't speak very good English," said Elfinn. "But come, what will you give me if I tell you?"

"If you tell me what?" said the tiresome prince.

"What you want to know."

"I don't want to know anything," said Prince Tiresome.

"Then you're more of a silly even than I thought," said Elfinn. "Don't you want to know how to settle the dragon before he settles you?"

"It might be as well," the prince admitted.

"Well, I haven't much patience at any time," said Elfinn, "and now I can assure you that there's very little left. What will you give me if I tell you?"

"Half my kingdom," said the prince, "and my cousin's hand in marriage."

"Done," said the pigkeeper. "Here goes! *The dragon grows small at nights!* He sleeps under the root of this tree. I use him to light my fire with."

And sure enough, there under the tree was the dragon on a nest of moss, and he was about as long as your finger.

"How can I kill him?" asked the prince.

"I don't know that you *can* kill him," said Elfinn, "but you can take him away if you've brought anything to put him in. That bottle of yours would do."

So between them they managed, with bits of stick and by singeing their fingers a little, to poke and shove the dragon till they made it creep into the silver hunting bottle, and then the prince screwed on the top tight.

"Now we've got him," said Elfinn, "let's take him home and put Solomon's seal on the mouth of the bottle, and then he'll be safe enough. Come along—we'll divide up the kingdom tomorrow, and then I shall have some money to buy fine clothes to go courting in."

But when the wicked prince made promises he did not make them to keep.

"Go on with you! What do you mean?" he said. "I found the dragon and I've imprisoned him. I never said a word about courtings or kingdoms. If you say I did, I shall cut your head off at once." And he drew his sword.

"All right," said Elfinn, shrugging his shoulders. "I'm better off than you are, anyhow."

"What do you mean?" spluttered the prince.

"Why, you've only got a kingdom (and a dragon), but I've got clean hands (and seventy-five fine black pigs)."

So Elfinn sat down again by his fire, and the prince went home and told his Parliament how clever and brave he had been, and though he woke them on purpose to tell them, they were not angry, but said, "You are indeed brave and clever." For they knew what happened to people with whom the prince was not pleased.

Then the prime minister solemnly put Solomon's seal on the mouth of the bottle, and the bottle was put in the treasury, which was the strongest building in the town, and was made of solid copper, with walls as thick as Waterloo Bridge.

The bottle was set down among the sacks of gold, and the junior secretary to the junior clerk of the last lord of the treasury was appointed to sit up all night with it, and see if anything happened. The junior secretary had never seen a dragon, and what was more, he did not believe the prince had ever seen a dragon either. The prince had never been a really truthful boy, and it would have been just like him to bring home a bottle with nothing in it, and then to pretend that there was a dragon inside. So the junior secretary did not at all mind being left.

They gave him the key, and when everyone in the town had gone back to bed he let in some of the junior secretaries from other government departments, and they had a jolly game of hide-and-seek among the sacks of gold, and played marbles with the diamonds and rubies and pearls in the big ivory chests.

They enjoyed themselves very much, but by and by the copper treasury began to get warmer and warmer, and suddenly the junior secretary cried out, "Look at the bottle!"

The bottle sealed with Solomon's seal had swollen to three times its proper size, and seemed to be nearly red hot, and the air got warmer and warmer and the bottle bigger and bigger, till all the junior secretaries agreed that the place was too hot to hold them, and out they went, tumbling over each other in their haste, and just as the last got out and locked the door the bottle burst, and out came the dragon, very fiery, and swelling more and more every minute, and he began to eat the sacks of gold, and crunch up the pearls and diamonds and rubies, as you do "hundreds and thousands.[1]"

By breakfast time he had devoured the whole of the prince's treasures, and when the prince came along the street at about eleven, he met the dragon coming out of the broken door of the treasury, with molten gold still dripping from his jaws. Then the prince turned and ran for his life, and as he ran towards the dragonproof tower the

[1]*Sweets like small shot for decorating cakes, etc.*

little white princess saw him coming, and she ran down and unlocked the door and let him in, and slammed the dragonproof door in the fiery face of the dragon, who sat down and whined outside, because he wanted the prince very much indeed.

The princess took Prince Tiresome into the best room, and laid the cloth, and gave him cream and eggs and white grapes and honey and bread, with many other things, yellow and white and good to eat. And she served him just as kindly as she would have done if he had been anyone else instead of the bad prince who had taken away her kingdom and kept it for himself —because she was a true princess and had a heart of gold.

When he had eaten and drunk he begged the princess to show him how to lock and unlock the door, and the nurse was asleep, so there was no one to tell the princess not to, and she did.

"You turn the key like this," she said, "and the door keeps shut. But turn it nine times round the wrong way, and the door flies open."

And so it did. And the moment it opened, the prince pushed the white princess out of her tower, just as he had pushed her out of her kingdom, and shut the door. For he wanted to have the tower all for himself. And there she was in the street, and on the other side of the way the dragon was sitting whining, but he did not try to eat her, because—though the old nurse did not know it—dragons cannot eat white princesses with hearts of gold.

The princess could not walk through the streets of the town in her milky-silky gown with

the daisies on it, and with no hat and no gloves,
so she turned the other way and ran out across
the meadows, towards the wood. She had never
been out of her tower before, and the soft grass
under her feet felt like grass of paradise.

She ran right into the thickest part of the
wood, because she did not know what her heart
was made of, and she was afraid of the dragon,
and there in a dell she came on Elfinn and his
seventy-five fine pigs. He was playing his flute,
and around him the pigs were dancing cheerfully
on their hind legs.

"Oh, dear," said the princess, "do take care
of me. I am so frightened."

"I will," said Elfinn, putting his arms round
her. "Now you are quite safe. What were you
frightened of?"

"The dragon," she said.

"So it's got out of the silver bottle," said
Elfinn. "I hope it's eaten the prince."

"No," said Sabrinetta. "But why?"

So he told her of the mean trick that the prince
had played him.

"And he promised me half his kingdom and
the hand of his cousin the princess," said Elfinn.

"Oh, dear, what a shame!" said Sabrinetta,
trying to get out of his arms. "How dared he?"

"What's the matter?" he asked, holding her
tighter. "It *was* a shame, or at least I thought so.
But *now* he may keep his kingdom, half and
whole, if I may keep what I have."

"What's that?" asked the princess.

"Why, you—my pretty, my dear," said
Elfinn. "And as for the princess, his cousin—
forgive me, dearest heart, but when I asked for

her I hadn't seen the real princess, the only princess, *my* princess."

"Do you mean me?" said Sabrinetta.

"Who else?" he asked.

"Yes, but five minutes ago you hadn't seen me!"

"Five minutes ago I was a pigkeeper—now I've held you in my arms I'm a prince, though I should have to keep pigs to the end of my days."

"But you haven't asked me," said the princess.

"*You* asked *me* to take care of you," said Elfinn, "and I will—all my life long."

So that was settled, and they began to talk of really important things, such as the dragon and the prince, and all the time Elfinn did not know that this was the princess, but he knew that she had a heart of gold: and he told her so, many times.

"The mistake," said Elfinn, "was in not having a dragonproof bottle. I see that now."

"Oh, is that all?" said the princess. "I can easily get you one of those—because everything in my tower is dragonproof. We ought to do something to settle the dragon and save the little children."

So she started off to get the bottle, and she would not let Elfinn come with her.

"If what you say is true," she said, "if you are sure that I have a heart of gold, the dragon won't hurt me, and somebody *must* stay with the pigs."

Elfinn was quite sure, so he let her go.

She found the door of her tower open. The dragon had waited patiently for the prince, and the moment he opened the door and came out, though he was only out for an instant to post a letter to his prime minister, saying where he was and asking them to send the fire brigade to deal with the fiery dragon, the dragon ate him. Then the dragon went back to the wood, because it was getting near his time to grow small for the night.

So Sabrinetta went in and kissed her nurse, and made her a cup of tea and explained what was going to happen, and that she had a heart of gold, so the dragon couldn't eat her. And the nurse saw that, of course, the princess was quite safe, and kissed her and let her go.

She took the dragonproof bottle, made of burnished brass, and ran back to the wood, and to the dell where Elfinn was sitting among his sleek black pigs, waiting for her.

"I thought you were never coming back," he said. "You have been away a year, at least."

The princess sat down beside him among the pigs, and they held each other's hands till it was dark, and then the dragon came crawling over the moss, scorching it as he came, and getting smaller as he crawled, and curled up under the root of the tree.

"Now, then," said Elfinn, "you hold the bottle." Then he poked and prodded the dragon with bits of stick till it crawled into the dragonproof bottle. But there was no stopper.

"Never mind," said Elfinn. "I'll put my finger in for a stopper."

"No, let me," said the princess, but of course Elfinn would not let her. He stuffed his finger into the top of the bottle, and the princess cried out, "The sea—the sea—run for the cliffs!" And off they went, with the seventy-five pigs trotting steadily after them in a long, black procession.

The bottle got hotter and hotter in Elfinn's hands, because the dragon inside was puffing fire and smoke with all his might. Hotter, and hotter, and hotter, but Elfinn held on till they came to the cliff edge, and there was the dark blue sea, and the whirlpool going round and round.

Elfinn lifted the bottle high above his head and hurled it out between the stars and the sea, and it fell in the middle of the whirlpool.

"We've saved the country," said the princess. "You've saved the little children. Give me your hands."

"I can't," said Elfinn. "I shall never be able to take your dear hands again. My hands are burned off."

And so they were: there were only black cinders where his hands ought to have been. The princess kissed them, and cried over them, and tore pieces of her silky-milky gown to tie them up with, and the two went back to the tower and told the nurse all about everything. And the pigs sat outside and waited.

"He is the bravest man in the world," said Sabrinetta. "He has saved the country and the little children, but oh, his hands—his poor, dear, darling hands!"

Here the door of the room opened, and the oldest of the seventy-five pigs came in. It went up to Elfinn and rubbed itself against him with little, loving grunts.

"See the dear creature," said the nurse, wiping away a tear. "It knows, it knows!"

Sabrinetta stroked the pig, because Elfinn had no hands for stroking or for anything else.

"The only cure for a dragon burn," said the old nurse, "is pig's fat, and well that faithful creature knows it."

"I wouldn't for a kingdom," cried Elfinn, stroking the pig as best he could with his elbow.

"Is there no other cure?" asked the princess.

Here another pig put its black nose in at the door, and then another and another, till the room was full of pigs, a surging mass of rounded blackness pushing and struggling to get at Elfinn, and grunting softly in the language of true affection.

"There is *one* other," said the nurse. "The dear, affectionate beasts—they all want to die for you."

"What *is* the other cure?" said Sabrinetta, anxiously.

"If a man is burned by a dragon," said the nurse, "and a certain number of people are willing to die for him, it is enough if each should kiss the burn, and wish it well in the depths of his loving heart."

"The number! The number!" cried Sabrinetta.

"Seventy-seven," said the nurse.

"We have only seventy-five pigs," said the princess, "and with me that's seventy-six!"

"It must be seventy-seven—and I really *can't* die for him, so nothing can be done," said the nurse, sadly. "He must have cork hands."

"I knew about the seventy-seven loving people," said Elfinn. "But I never thought my dear pigs loved me so much as all this, and my

134

dear, too. And of course, that only makes it more impossible. There's *one* other charm that cures dragon burns, though, but I'd rather be burned black all over than marry anyone but you, my dear, my pretty."

"Why, who must you marry to cure your dragon burns?" asked Sabrinetta.

"A princess. That's how St. George cured *his* burns."

"There now! Think of that!" said the nurse. "And I never heard tell of that cure, old as I am."

But Sabrinetta threw her arms round Elfinn's neck, and held him as though she would never let him go.

"Then it's all right, my dear, brave, precious Elfinn," she cried, "for I *am* a princess, and you shall be my prince. Come along, Nurse—don't wait to put on your bonnet. We'll go and be married this very moment."

So they went, and the pigs came after, moving in stately blackness, two by two. And the minute he was married to the princess, Elfinn's hands got quite well. And the people, who were weary of Prince Tiresome and his hippopotamuses, hailed Sabrinetta and her husband as rightful sovereigns of the land.

Next morning the prince and princess went out to see if the dragon had been washed ashore. They could see nothing of him, but when they looked out towards the whirlpool they saw a cloud of steam, and the fishermen reported that the water for miles round was hot enough to shave with! And as the water is hot there to this day, we may feel pretty sure that the fierceness of that dragon was such that all the waters of all the seas were not enough to cool him. The whirlpool is too strong for him to be able to get out of it, so there he spins round and round for ever and ever, doing some useful work at last, and warming the water for poor fisherfolk to shave with.

The prince and princess rule the land well and wisely. The nurse lives with them, and does nothing but fine sewing, and only that when she wants to very much. The prince keeps no hippopotamuses, and is consequently very popular. The seventy-five devoted pigs live in white marble sties with brass knockers and "Pig" on the doorplate, and are washed twice a day with Turkish sponges and soap scented with violets. And no one objects to *their* following the prince when he walks abroad, for they behave beautifully, and always keep to the footpath, and obey the notices about not walking on the grass. The princess feeds them every day with her own hands, and her first edict on coming to the throne was that the word *pork* should never be uttered on pain of death, and should, besides, be scratched out of all the dictionaries.

Chapter 8

*Kind Little Edmund, or
the Caves and the Cockatrice*

Edmund was a boy. The people who did not like
him said that he was the most tiresome boy that
ever lived, but his grandmother and his other
friends said that he had an inquiring mind. And
his granny often added that he was the best of
boys. But she was very kind and very old.

Edmund loved to find out about things.
Perhaps you will think that in that case he was
constant in his attendance at school, since there,
if anywhere, we may learn whatever there is to
be learned. But Edmund did not want to learn
things: he wanted to find things out, which is
quite different. His inquiring mind led him to
take clocks to pieces to see what made them go,
to take locks off doors to see what made them
stick. It was Edmund who cut open the india
rubber ball to see what made it bounce, and he
never *did* see, any more than you did when you
tried the same experiment.

Edmund lived with his grandmother. She loved him very much, in spite of his inquiring mind, and hardly scolded him at all when he frizzled up her tortoiseshell comb in his anxiety to find out whether it was made of real tortoiseshell or of something that would burn. Edmund went to school, of course, now and then, and sometimes he could not prevent himself from learning something, but he never did it on purpose.

"It is such waste of time," said he. "They only know what everybody knows. I want to find out new things that nobody has thought of but me."

"I don't think you're likely to find out anything that none of the wise men in the whole world have thought of all these thousands of years," said granny.

But Edmund did not agree with her. He played truant whenever he could, for he was a kindhearted boy, and could not bear to think of a master's time and labor being thrown away on a boy like himself—who did not wish to learn, only to find out—when there were so many worthy lads thirsting for instruction in geography and history, and reading and ciphering, and Mr. Smiles's *Self-Help*.

Other boys played truant too, of course— and these went nutting or blackberrying or wild-plum gathering, but Edmund never went on the side of the town where the green woods and hedges grew. He always went up the mountain where the great rocks were, and the tall, dark pine trees, and where other people were afraid to go because of the strange noises that came out of the caves.

Edmund was not afraid of these noises—though they were very strange and terrible. He wanted to find out what made them. And one day he did. He had invented, all by himself, a very ingenious and new kind of lantern, made with a turnip and a tumbler, and when he had taken the candle out of granny's bedroom candlestick to put it in, it gave quite a splendid light.

He had to go to school next day, and he was caned for being absent without leave—although he very straightforwardly explained that he had been too busy making the lantern to have time to come to school.

But the day after he got up very early, and took the lunch granny had got ready for him to take to school—two boiled eggs and an apple turnover—and he took his lantern and went off as straight as a dart to the mountains to explore the caves.

The caves were very dark, but his lantern lighted them up beautifully. And they were most interesting caves, with stalactites and stalagmites and fossils, and all the things you read about in the instructive books for the young. But Edmund did not care for any of these things just then. He wanted to find out what made the noises that people were afraid of, and there was nothing in the caves to tell him.

Presently he sat down in the biggest cave and listened very carefully, and it seemed to him that he could distinguish three different sorts of noises. There was a heavy, rumbling sound, like a very large old gentleman asleep after dinner; and there was a smaller sort of rumble going on at the same time; and there was a sort of crowing, clucking sound, such as a chicken might make if it happened to be as big as a haystack.

"It seems to me," said Edmund to himself, "that the clucking is nearer than the others." So he started up again and explored the caves once more. He found out nothing, only, about halfway up the wall of the cave, he saw a hole. And being a boy, he climbed up to it and crept in, and it was the entrance to a rocky passage. And now the clucking sounded more plainly than before, and he could hardly hear the rumbling at all.

"I am going to find out something at last," said Edmund, and on he went. The passage wound and twisted, and twisted and turned, and turned and wound, but Edmund kept on.

"My lantern's burning better and better," said he presently, but the next minute he saw that all the light did not come from his lantern. It was a pale yellow light, and it shone down the passage far ahead of him through what looked like the chink of a door.

"I expect it's the fire in the middle of the earth," said Edmund, who had not been able to help learning about that at school.

But quite suddenly the fire ahead gave a pale flicker and went down, and the clucking ceased.

The next moment Edmund turned a corner and found himself in front of a rocky door. The door was ajar. He went in, and there was a round cave, like the dome of St. Paul's. In the middle of the cave was a hole like a very big wash-hand basin, and in the middle of the basin Edmund saw a large pale person sitting. This person had a man's face and a griffin's body, and big, feathery wings, and a snake's tail, and a cock's comb and neck feathers.

"Whatever are you?" said Edmund.

"I'm a poor starving cockatrice," answered the

pale person, in a very faint voice, "and I shall die—oh, I know I shall! My fire's gone out. I can't think how it happened; I must have been asleep. I have to stir it seven times round with my tail once in a hundred years to keep it alight, and my watch must have been wrong. And now I shall die."

I think I have said before what a kindhearted boy Edmund was.

"Cheer up," said he. "I'll light your fire for you," and off he went, and in a few minutes he came back with a great armful of sticks from the pine trees outside, and with these and a lesson book or two that he had forgotten to lose before, and which, quite by an oversight, were safe in his pocket, he lighted a fire all round the cockatrice. The wood blazed up, and presently something in the basin caught fire, and Edmund saw that it was a sort of liquid that burned like the brandy in a snapdragon. And now the cockatrice stirred it with his tail, and flapped his wings in it, so that some of it splashed out on Edmund's hand and burned it rather badly. But the cockatrice grew red and strong and happy, and its comb grew scarlet, and its feathers glossy, and it lifted itself up and crowed, "Cock-a-trice-a-doodle-doo!" very loudly and clearly.

Edmund's kindly nature was charmed to see the cockatrice so much improved in health, and he said, "Don't mention it; delighted, I'm sure," when the cockatrice began to thank him.

"But what can I do for you?" said the creature.

"Tell me stories," said Edmund.

"What about?" said the cockatrice.

"About true things that they don't know at school," said Edmund.

So the cockatrice began, and it told him about mines and treasures, and geological formations, and about gnomes and fairies and dragons, and glaciers and the Stone Age, and the beginning of the world, and about the unicorn and the phoenix, and about magic, black and white.

And Edmund ate his eggs and his turnover, and listened. And when he got hungry again he said good-bye and went home. But he came again next day for more stories, and the next day, and the next, for a long time.

He told the boys at school about the cockatrice and its wonderful true tales, and the boys liked the stories, but when he told the master he was caned for untruthfulness.

"But it's true," said Edmund. "Just you look where the fire burned my hand."

"I see you've been playing with fire—in mischief as usual," said the master, and he caned Edmund harder than ever. The master was ignorant and unbelieving, but I am told that some schoolmasters are not like that.

Now, one day Edmund made a new lantern out of something chemical which he sneaked from the school laboratory. And with it he went exploring again to see if he could find the things that made the other sorts of noises. And in quite another part of the mountain he found a dark passage, all lined with brass, so that it was like the inside of a huge telescope, and at the very end of it he found a bright green door. There was a brass plate on the door which said, "Mrs. D. Knock and ring," and a white label which said, "Call me at three."

Edmund had a watch. It had been given to him on his birthday two days before, and he had not yet had time to take it to pieces and see what made it go, so it was still going. He looked at it now. It said a quarter to three.

Did I tell you before what a kindhearted boy Edmund was? He sat down on the brass doorstep and waited till three o'clock. Then he knocked and rang, and there was a rattling and puffing inside. The great door flew open, and Edmund had only just time to hide behind it when out came an immense yellow dragon and wriggled off down the brass cave, like a long, rattling worm—or perhaps more like a monstrous centipede.

Edmund crept slowly out, and saw the dragon stretching herself on the rocks in the sun, and he crept past the great creature and tore down the hill into the town and burst into school, crying out, ''There's a great dragon coming! Somebody ought to do something, or we shall all be destroyed.''

He was caned for untruthfulness without any delay. His master was never one for postponing a duty.

''But it's *true*,'' said Edmund. ''You just see if it isn't.''

He pointed out of the window, and everyone could see a vast yellow cloud rising up into the air above the mountain.

''It's only a thunder shower,'' said the master, and caned Edmund more than ever. This master was not like some masters I know: he was very obstinate, and would not believe his own eyes if they told him anything different from what he had been saying before his eyes spoke.

So while the master was writing ''Lying is very wrong, and liars must be caned. It is all for their own good'' on the blackboard for Edmund to copy out seven hundred times, Edmund sneaked out of school and ran for his life across the town to warn his granny, but she was not at home. So then he made off by the back door of the town, and raced up the hill to tell the cockatrice, and ask for its help. It never occurred to him that the cockatrice might not believe him. You see, he had heard so many wonderful tales from it and had believed them all—and when you believe all a person's stories they ought to believe yours. This is only fair.

At the mouth of the cockatrice's cave Edmund stopped, very much out of breath, to look back at the town. As he ran he had felt his little legs tremble and shake, while the shadows of the great yellow cloud fell upon him. Now he stood once more between warm earth and blue sky, and looked down on the green plain, dotted with fruit trees and red-roofed farms and plots of gold corn. In the middle of that plain the gray town lay, with its strong walls, with the holes pierced for the archers, and its square towers with holes in for dropping melted lead on the heads of strangers, its bridges, and its steeples, the quiet river edged with willow and alder, and the pleasant green garden place in the middle of the town, where people sat on holidays to smoke their pipes and listen to the band.

Edmund saw it all. And he saw, too, creeping across the plain, marking her way by a black line, as everything withered at her touch, the great yellow dragon—and he saw that she was many times bigger than the whole town.

''Oh, my poor, dear granny,'' said Edmund, for he had a feeling heart, as I ought to have told you before.

The yellow dragon crept nearer and nearer, licking her greedy lips with her long, red tongue, and Edmund knew that in the school his master was still teaching earnestly, and still not believing Edmund's tale the least little bit.

"He'll jolly well *have* to believe it soon, anyhow," said Edmund to himself, and though he was a very tenderhearted boy—I think it only fair to tell you that he was this—I am afraid he was not so sorry as he ought to have been to think of the way in which his master was going to learn how to believe what Edmund said. Then the dragon opened her jaws wider and wider and wider. Edmund shut his eyes close, for though his master *was* in the town, yet the amiable Edmund shrank from beholding the awful sight.

When he opened his eyes again there was no town—only a bare place where it had stood, and the dragon licking her lips and curling herself up to go to sleep, just as pussy does when she has quite finished with a mouse. Edmund gasped once or twice, and then ran into the cave to tell the cockatrice.

"Well," said the cockatrice, thoughtfully, when the tale had been told, "what then?"

"I don't think you quite understand," said Edmund, gently. "The dragon has swallowed up the town."

"Does it matter?" said the cockatrice.

"But I live there," said Edmund, blankly.

"Never mind," said the cockatrice, turning over in the pool of fire to warm its other side, which was chilly, because Edmund had, as usual, forgotten to close the cave door, "you can live here with me."

"I'm afraid I haven't made my meaning clear," said Edmund, patiently. "You see, my granny is in the town, and I can't bear to lose my granny like this."

"I don't know what a granny may be," said the cockatrice, who seemed to be growing weary of the subject, "but if it's a possession to which you attach any importance—"

"Of course it is," said Edmund, losing patience at last. "Oh—do help me. What can I do?"

"If I were you," said his friend, stretching itself out in the pool of flame so that the waves covered it up to the chin, "I should find the drakling and bring it here."

"But why?" said Edmund. He had got into the habit of asking why at school, and the master had always found it trying. As for the cockatrice, it was not going to stand that sort of thing for a moment.

"Oh, don't talk to me!" it said, splashing angrily in the flames. "I give you advice, take it or leave it—I shan't bother about you anymore. If you bring the drakling here to me, I'll tell you what to do next. If not, not."

And the cockatrice drew the fire up close round its shoulders, tucked itself up in it, and went to sleep.

Now this was exactly the right way to manage Edmund, only no one had ever thought of trying to do it before.

He stood for a moment looking at the cockatrice. It looked at him out of the corner of its eye and began to snore very loud, and Edmund understood, once and for all, that it wasn't going to put up with any nonsense. He respected the cockatrice very much from that moment, and set off at once to do exactly as he was told—for perhaps the first time in his life.

Though he had played truant so often, he knew one or two things that perhaps you don't know, though you have always been so good and gone to school regularly. For instance, he knew that a drakling is a dragon's baby, and he felt sure that what he had to do was to find the third of the three noises that people used to hear coming from the mountains. Of course, the clucking had been the cockatrice, and the big noise like a large gentleman asleep after dinner had been the big dragon. So the smaller rumbling must have been the drakling.

He plunged boldly into the caves, and searched and wandered and wandered and searched, and at last he came to a third door in the mountain, and on it was written, "The baby is asleep." Just before the door stood fifty pairs of copper shoes, and no one could have looked at them for a moment without seeing what sort of feet they were made for, for each shoe had five holes in it for the drakling's five claws. And there were fifty pairs, because the drakling took after his mother and had a hundred feet—no more and no less. He was the kind called *Draco centipedis* in the learned books.

Edmund was a good deal frightened, but he remembered the grim expression of the cockatrice's eye, and the fixed determination of its snore still rang in his ears, in spite of the snoring of the drakling, which was, in itself, considerable.

He screwed up his courage, flung the door open, and called out, "Halloa, you drakling. Get out of bed this minute."

The drakling stopped snoring and said sleepily, "It ain't time yet."

"Your mother says you are to, anyhow. And look sharp about it, what's more," said Edmund, gaining courage from the fact that the drakling had not yet eaten him.

The drakling sighed, and Edmund could hear it getting out of bed. The next moment it began to come out of its room and to put on its shoes. It was not nearly so big as its mother—only about the size of a Baptist chapel.

"Hurry up," said Edmund, as it fumbled clumsily with the seventeenth shoe.

"Mother said I was never to go out without my shoes," said the drakling, so Edmund had to help it to put them on. It took some time, and was not a comfortable occupation.

At last the drakling said it was ready, and Edmund, who had forgotten to be frightened, said, "Come on then," and they went back to the cockatrice.

The cave was rather narrow for the drakling, but it made itself thin, as you may see a fat worm do when it wants to get through a narrow crack in a piece of hard earth.

"Here it is," said Edmund, and the cockatrice woke up at once and asked the drakling very politely to sit down and wait. "Your mother will be here presently," said the cockatrice, stirring up its fire.

The drakling sat down and waited, but it watched the fire with hungry eyes.

"I beg your pardon," it said at last, "but I am always accustomed to have a little basin of fire directly after I get up, and I feel rather faint. Might I?"

It reached out a claw towards the cockatrice's basin.

"Certainly not," said the cockatrice sharply. "Where were you brought up? Did they never teach you that 'we must not ask for all we see'? Eh?"

"I beg your pardon," said the drakling humbly. "But I am really very hungry."

The cockatrice beckoned Edmund to the side of the basin and whispered in his ear so long and so earnestly that one side of the dear boy's hair was quite burned off. And he never once interrupted the cockatrice to ask why.

But when the whispering was over, Edmund— whose heart, as I may have mentioned, was very tender—said to the drakling, "If you are really hungry, poor thing, I can show you where there is plenty of fire." And off he went through the caves, and the drakling followed.

When Edmund came to the proper place he stopped.

There was a round iron thing in the floor, like the ones the men shoot the coals down into your cellar, only much larger. Edmund heaved it up by a hook that stuck out at one side, and a rush of hot air came up that nearly choked him.

But the drakling came close, and looked down with one eye, and sniffed, and said, "That smells good, eh?"

"Yes," said Edmund. "Well, that's the fire in the middle of the earth. There's plenty of it, all done to a turn. You'd better go down and begin your breakfast, hadn't you?"

So the drakling wriggled through the hole, and began to crawl faster and faster down the slanting shaft that leads to the fire in the middle of the earth. And Edmund, doing exactly as he had been told, for a wonder, caught the end of the drakling's tail, and ran the iron hook through it, so that the drakling was held fast. And it could not turn round and wriggle up again to look after its poor tail, because, as everyone knows, the way to the fires below is very easy to go down, but quite impossible to come back on. There is something about it in Latin, beginning, *Facilis descensus*.

So there was the drakling, fast by the silly tail of it, and there was Edmund very busy and important, and very pleased with himself, hurrying back to the cockatrice.

"Now," said he.

"Well, now," said it, "go to the mouth of the cave and laugh at the dragon so that she hears you."

Edmund very nearly said "Why?" but he stopped in time and instead said, "She won't hear me—"

"Oh, very well," said the cockatrice. "No doubt you know best." And it began to tuck itself up again in the fire, so Edmund did as he was bid.

And when he began to laugh his laughter echoed in the mouth of the cave till it sounded like the laughter of a whole castleful of giants.

And the dragon, lying asleep in the sun, woke up and said very crossly, "What are you laughing at?"

"At you," said Edmund, and went on laughing. The dragon bore it as long as she could, but like everyone else, she couldn't stand being made fun of, so presently she dragged herself up the mountain very slowly, because she had just had a rather heavy meal, and stood outside, and said, "What are you laughing at?" in a voice that made Edmund feel as if he should never laugh again.

Then the good cockatrice called out, "At *you!* You've eaten your own drakling—swallowed it with the town. Your own little drakling! He, he, he! Ha, ha, ha!''

And Edmund found courage to cry "Ha, ha!" which sounded like tremendous laughter in the echo of the cave.

"Dear me," said the dragon. "I thought the town stuck in my throat rather. I must take it out, and look through it more carefully." And with that she coughed—and choked—and there was the town on the hillside.

Edmund had run back to the cockatrice, and it had told him what to do. So before the dragon had time to look through the town again for her drakling, the voice of the drakling itself was heard howling miserably from inside the mountain, because Edmund was pinching its tail as hard as he could in the round iron door, like the one where the men pour the coals out of the sacks into the cellar.

And the dragon heard the voice and said, "Why, whatever's the matter with baby? He's *not* here!" and made herself thin, and crept into the mountain to find her drakling. The cockatrice kept on laughing as loud as it could, and Edmund kept on pinching, and presently the great dragon—very long and narrow she had made herself—found her head where the round hole was with the iron lid. Her tail was a mile or two off—outside the mountain. When Edmund heard her coming he gave one last nip to the drakling's tail, and then heaved up the lid and stood behind it, so that the dragon could not see him. Then he loosed the drakling's tail from the hook, and the dragon peeped down the hole just in time to see her drakling's tail disappear down the smooth, slanting shaft with one last squeak of pain. Whatever may have been the poor dragon's other faults, she was an excellent mother. She plunged head first into the hole, and slid down the shaft after her baby. Edmund watched her head go—and then the rest of her. She was so long, now she had stretched herself thin, that it took all night. It was like watching a goods train go by in Germany. When the last joint of her tail had gone Edmund slammed down the iron door. He was a kindhearted boy, as you have guessed, and he was glad to think that dragon and drakling would now have plenty to eat of their favorite food, forever and ever. He thanked the cockatrice for his kindness, and got home just in time to have breakfast and get to school by nine. Of course, he could not have done this if the town had been in its old place by the river in the middle of the plain, but it had taken root on the hillside just where the dragon left it.

"Well," said the master, "where were you yesterday?"

Edmund explained, and the master at once caned him for not speaking the truth.

"But it *is* true," said Edmund. "Why, the whole town was swallowed by the dragon. You know it was."

"Nonsense," said the master. "There was a thunderstorm and an earthquake, that's all."

And he caned Edmund more than ever.

"But," said Edmund, who always would argue, even in the least favorable circumstances, "how do you account for the town being on the hillside now, instead of by the river as it used to be?"

"It was *always* on the hillside," said the master. And all the class said the same, for they had more sense than to argue with a person who carried a cane.

"But look at the maps," said Edmund, who wasn't going to be beaten in argument, whatever he might be in the flesh. The master pointed to the map on the wall.

There was the town, *on the hillside!* And nobody but Edmund could see that of course the shock of being swallowed by the dragon had upset all the maps and put them wrong.

And then the master caned Edmund again, explaining that this time it was not for untruthfulness but for his vexatious argumentative habits. This will show you what a prejudiced and ignorant man Edmund's master was—how different from the revered head of the nice school where your good parents are kind enough to send you.

Next day Edmund thought he would prove his tale by showing people the cockatrice, and he actually persuaded some people to go into the cave with him, but the cockatrice had bolted itself in, and would not open the door. So Edmund got nothing by that except a scolding for taking people on a wild-goose chase.

"A wild goose," said they, "is nothing like a cockatrice."

And poor Edmund could not say a word, though he knew how wrong they were. The only person who believed him was his granny. But then she was very old and very kind, and had always said he was the best of boys.

Only one good thing came of all this long story. Edmund has never been quite the same boy since. He does not argue quite so much, and he agreed to be apprenticed to a locksmith, so that he might some day be able to pick the lock of the cockatrice's front door—and learn some more of the things that other people don't know.

But he is quite an old man now, and he hasn't got that door open yet!

About the author:
Edith Nesbit

Edith Nesbit, born in England in 1858, was a daring and mischievous child. She had many brothers and sisters, and drew upon their adventures for her later stories. Edith Nesbit was lifelong friends with George Bernard Shaw and H.G. Wells.